UNREGULATED CAPITALISM

Unregulated Capitalism is Destroying Democracy and the Economy

By

GEORGE GAASVIG

Attachments: Declaration of Independence; Constitution of the United States of America;
Share Our Wealth – Huey P. Long; Economic Bill of Rights – Franklin D. Roosevelt

ISBN-10: 1483980499
ISBN-13: 9781483980492
Library of Congress Control Number: 2013906001
CreateSpace Independent Publishing Platform
North Charleston, South Carolina

ABOUT THE AUTHOR

George Gaasvig was born February 22, 1945. He graduated with honors from Bemidji State University in Minnesota with degrees in business administration and industrial technology. He has worked in government, retail, construction, and consulting, has been self-employed, and is a certified property manager. He has served on national committees in the field of public and Indian housing. He has provided written testimony and testified before congressional committees. He has submitted reports for publication in congressional committee reports and the *Congressional Record*. He has participated in the creation of federal legislation and regulations.

FOREWORD

The opening sentence of the United States Constitution states: "We the people of the United States, in Order to form a more perfect Union, establish Justice, insure domestic Tranquility, provide for the common defence, promote the general Welfare, and secure the Blessings of Liberty to ourselves and our Posterity, do ordain and establish this Constitution for the United States of America." Unfortunately the wording "to ourselves and our Posterity" was derived of, by, and for the wealthy, elite aristocracy and not for working class Americans. The result is a democracy and economic system of, by, and for the wealthy, elite capitalists and large corporations in America. This is evident by the obscene disparity in income and wealth accumulation between the "haves" and have-nots" that exists today. When 89 percent of the wealth of the nation is concentrated in the richest 20 percent of citizens and only 11 percent of the wealth is held by the 80 percent of mostly working class and small business owners, the unfettered, unregulated capitalist economic system is not promoting the general welfare of working class Americans. What America and any democratic nation need are a true democracy and a fair and equitable economic system. This can be accomplished first and foremost by every citizen getting registered to vote and then voting his or her interests in every election, and secondly by elimination of the unfettered, unregulated capitalist economic system and replacing it with the adoption of a fair and equitable economic system.

A democracy is portrayed as government by the majority, fairness, and equal economic opportunity. When any nation evolves to the point where the government and a majority of the wealth of the nation are concentrated in the hands of less than 1 percent of the population, no longer is that nation a democracy. In fact, it is questionable whether that nation ever was a democracy, rather than a nation of, by, and for the wealthy that was only portrayed as a democracy. In any event, when 1 percent of the wealthy and corporate interests can use their wealth to buy the election or appointment of a majority of the government, from the Supreme Court justices to congressmen to the presidency to state governments, there is no longer any assimilation of a true democracy. This power quest and greed sickness to have everything unto themselves and let everyone else fend for themselves is undemocratic, unpatriotic, and un-American. It leaves a majority of Americans with needs that cannot be met, many without jobs, many in poverty, and most wondering what happened. It also destroys the economy and, if left unchecked, will destroy the government.

The element that allows for this hoarding of wealth and power is an unfettered, unregulated capitalist economic system. When this power- and greed-motivated element pursues the reduction of taxation on themselves, the deregulation of any and all controls on unfettered capitalism, the privatization of established government institutions and services, all in the quest for more profits, wealth, and power for themselves, the greedy get richer and the working class gets fleeced. It becomes obvious that something is wrong in such a nation, and what is wrong is the unfettered, unregulated capitalist economic system. The change that is needed when a nation reaches the point of everything for a few at the expense of the rest is a fair and equitable economic system that provides hope and opportunity for everyone. The economic system of fairness and equality for a true democracy is Social Capitalism with regulations. Social Capitalism requires that there are three equal parties in a democratic economy: the working class, government, and capitalists. The needs of all three parties must be addressed in order for a democratic economy to be fair and equitable. Capitalists must be provided a reasonable profit for their risks, the working class must be provided at least a living wage and affordable benefits, and the government must provide regulation over the inherent greed of capitalists and corporations. This book proposes the replacement of an unfettered, unregulated capitalist economic system with a regulated Social Capitalist economic system as adopted into law by government to be fair and equitable to all in a true democracy.

UNREGULATED CAPITALISM

Unregulated Capitalism is Destroying Democracy and the Economy

CONTENTS

Page

About the Author iii

Foreword v

Contents ix

Introduction xi

Definitions xxi

I   Democracy and Capitalism 1

II   Minority Government 17

III Social Capitalism 23

     1.   Democracy 27

     2.   Voting 32

         2.1   Two-Party Political System 37

         2.2   Statesmen/Stateswomen 44

         2.3   Voter Registration 46

         2.4   Voting Machines 48

         2.5   Electoral College 48

         2.6   Career Politicians/Term Limits 50

         2.7   Publicly Financed Campaigns 56

     3.   Taxation 59

     4.   National Defense 65

         4.1   Veterans 66

     5.   National Debt 69

     6.   Health Care 74

         6.1   National Health Care 75

         6.2   Medicare/Medicaid 78

         6.3   Regionalization 78

　　6.4　Cost Containment 80
　　6.5　Health Insurance...81
　7.　Employment 83
　　7.1　Full Employment Policy...88
　　7.2　Living Wage..93
　　7.3　Employment Incentives 95
　　7.4　Employment Tax Credits 102
　　7.5　Employees...103
　　7.6　Unions...106
　　7.7　Child Care..110
　8.　Education..111
　　8.1　Motivation in Education...113
　　8.2　Teacher Involvement...115
　　8.3　Business Education and Involvement 116
　　8.4　Higher Education Financing.....................................117
　9.　Social Security..119
　10.　Environment 123
　11.　Justice...131
　12.　Constitutional Convention 147

IV Summary..155

Appendix A　Declaration of Independence 167
Appendix B　Constitution of the United States of America.................173
Appendix C　Share Our Wealth—Huey P. Long 207
Appendix D　Economic Bill of Rights—Franklin D. Roosevelt..........209

"There are only two families in the world, the Haves and the Have-Nots."

—Cervantes

INTRODUCTION

The economic system of any nation, especially a democratic nation or nation wanting to become a democratic nation, must provide a manner of fairness and equality for all the nation's people. Unfettered capitalism as the economic system in a democracy does not provide fairness and equity for all. Unfettered, *laissez-faire*, unregulated capitalism is of, by, and for the rich, elite capitalists. Unfettered capitalism tends to subordinate the working class to a commodity to be used by the capitalists in their quest for profits and wealth accumulation. Unfettered capitalism is not a fair and equitable economic system. It is a license to steal for greedy capitalists and a practice of false hope for the working class. Unfettered capitalism must be replaced with Social Capitalism in order to provide fairness in economic opportunity for all.

Throughout history, there have always been two classes of people in the world, the "haves" and the "have-nots." Haves are the rich and elite, while the have-nots are the rest of the particular population. The two classes under a democracy and unfettered capitalist economic system are the capitalists and labor, or the working class. Daily life for many of the have-nots or working class is much more precarious than for the capitalists. The precariousness is exaggerated substantially when there is an organized effort to create a very powerful and controlling capitalist class and a subordinated working class.

When a nation proclaiming democracy for all is created and the population is mandated to join a "civilized society," the government of that democratic nation is equally mandated to ensure fair and equitable treatment of all the people. Such is not the case with unfettered capitalism as the economic system. Unfettered capitalism unfairly favors the rich, elite capitalists over the working class. Is unfettered capitalism the best economic system for a democratic nation? The answer is "absolutely not."

Capitalism as an economic system in and of itself is not the culprit. The culprit is an economic system of *laissez-faire*, unfettered, unregulated capitalism coupled with the inherent greed of man. Greed can be an addiction or sickness similar to alcohol or drugs. Greed is the quest for wealth that is way beyond reason or need and must therefore be regulated. This is the failing of unfettered capitalism.

Human psychology has taught us that different people have different personality profiles. Personality profile tests have shown that there are several human attributes that impel people in various directions. Some people by nature are introverted; others are extroverted. Some people can be compassionate, while others are greedy. Some are planners and others are doers. When those people with certain attributes like greed become intolerant of others with differing attributes, the attribute must be regulated for the betterment of all in a civilized society. Such is the case with the greed inherent in an unfettered capitalism economic system. The greed must be regulated by replacing unfettered capitalism with Social Capitalism as the fair and equitable economic system for democracy.

Capitalists do not believe that the privilege of private ownership of the means of production and distribution under unfettered capitalism carries with it a social responsibility. They do not believe they are to be held responsible to ensure that the working class is provided a decent standard of living through employment opportunities at a living wage and living benefits. This belief is fueled by greed.

Unfettered capitalism theory must be revisited to come up with a balanced economic system. Capitalism is not all wrong; it just needs good, enforceable regulation. This is exactly what is wrong with unfettered capitalism, and it is long overdue for change. Not all capitalists are greedy. In fact, some capitalists and corporations have outstanding records of providing for their working-class employees. Unfortunately, these are exceptions rather than the rule as it should be.

The fuel of a nation's economy is not capital from the capitalists, as capitalists would like everyone to believe. The fuel that drives an economy is the labor of the working class. Throughout history, the false belief that as the rich, powerful, elite aristocracy goes, so goes a nation, has resulted in the destruction of nearly every nation or civilization. Fair compensation to the working class via a living wage and benefits results in the working class spending their wages to buy the products produced, and the nation prospers. When greedy capitalists hoard capital unto themselves, shield their obscene profits from taxation, refuse to pay fair wages to the working class, refuse the working class fair benefits for their labor, like health care and retirement, and organize to maintain power, profits, and wealth at all costs, a nation's economy does not prosper and the nation suffers. Large multinational corporations that perpetrate profits, wealth, and greed at all costs include oil companies, "too big to fail" banks, insurance companies, hedge fund companies, private equity companies, and pharmaceutical companies.

In a society which is void of a balanced economic system, the greed, money, and power of the capitalists can overwhelm fairness and respect for the working class. When this happens, governments controlled by minority capitalists can end up setting the policy for all. Many times, this policy is not in the interest of the nation, and therefore the people of the majority working class must speak up. However, the majority must be led by those who have integrity and the interests of the majority at heart. In addition, those who would lead must have the proper basis from which to effect change. The proper basis is not an unfettered capitalist economic system. The proper basis for a civilized democracy is Social Capitalism.

A balanced economic system that would hold capitalists socially responsible would be "Social Capitalism." Social Capitalism allows capitalists to have the privilege of capital accumulation and private ownership of the means of production and distribution, but also mandates that the capitalists provide social responsibility through living wages, health care, pensions, day care, etc., for the working class. In return for the mandate of social responsibility, tax policy must be revised to provide tax credits to the capitalists/corporations and businesses for being socially responsible.

As with all other dynamic aspects of a society, the economic system must be reviewed and corrected as time goes on to ensure a balance is afforded all the people. This has not happened with unfettered capitalism. Unfettered capitalist economic theory seems to have been etched in stone and therefore remains unchallenged. Therefore, correction of the economic system mutually eliminates, corrects, or significantly improves many other problems faced by a civilized society. A better economic system for democracy is Social Capitalism. "Social" is to ensure a decent standard of living for the working class, and "Capitalism," along with a balanced social responsibility, is for capitalists. Social Capitalism mutually includes the government that must enact the legislation and regulation necessary to regulate a balanced economic system and especially to control greed. However, if the government is made up of and controlled by the greedy capitalists, a socially balanced economic system will not happen. The only chance for a socially balanced economic system is for the government to be controlled by the majority working class.

For example, in America over the years, others have tried in different ways to improve the living standard for working class Americans. President Abraham Lincoln was assassinated for his belief that emancipated slaves should be given the right to vote. Senator Huey P. Long of Louisiana was murdered for his plan to "Share Our Wealth" (appendix C). President Franklin D. Roosevelt died in office before he could get his "Economic Bill of Rights" (Appendix D) passed by Congress. Democratic President John F. Kennedy was assassinated in office. Dr. Martin Luther King, Jr., who advocated for a nonviolent civil rights movement, was murdered. There seems to be a pattern that speaking out for equitable economic rights for the working class in America will not be tolerated by capitalists or the advocates of unfettered capitalism. In addition, America has several profound documents that have proven to be instrumental in setting its course in history. Among these documents are the Declaration of Independence and the Constitution of the United States of America (see appendices A and B, respectively). Each of these has proven to be an inextinguishable beacon in the quest for democracy, equality, and man's interaction with man. However, as profound as these documents are, there are parts missing. Both documents tend to address the intended equality and fairness in a democracy when, in fact, the unfettered capitalist economic system in America has evolved to grossly favor the capitalists at the expense of the working class, thus creating an unbalanced economic system. The essence of this book is to show that *laissez-faire*, unregulated, unfettered capitalism is wrong for a democracy. A better economic system for America is Social Capitalism.

The solutions offered in this book address the issue of social responsibility. In addition, solutions to other problems that result from unfettered capitalism will be offered. The status quo is no longer acceptable. Solutions must be carried out, not trivialized and discarded, if problems are to be resolved. For change to happen, the working class must take control of the government by exercising the right and duty to vote. Regardless of the economic system in a democracy, a democracy still insists that the people, as voters and taxpayers, get involved in their government.

The discussion of democracy and a Social Capitalist economic system throughout this book will be based on the democracy and Constitution of the United States of America as a model. The recognition and adoption of a Social Capitalist economic system would significantly change the model to include a greater participation by and recognition of the working class in the political and economic systems. Although the model is from America, the applications and recommendations for change would be applicable for any nation wishing to establish or improve democracy to include a Social Capitalism economic system in place of an unfettered capitalist economic system.

There are many solutions to problems or changes that would benefit a nation's democracy with the adoption of a Social Capitalist economic system. The implementation of a Social Capitalist economic system would solve many problems and have numerous benefits for a nation's democracy. These would include:

- Social Capitalism would establish a three-party economic partnership of working class labor, capitalists, and the government.

- Working class jobs are the fuel of a thriving economy.

- The greatest asset of any business is the brains of employees.

- Establish a full employment policy through taxation of the private sector with employment tax credits afforded the capitalists, corporations, and businesses that provide their employees with a living wage and living benefits.

- Replace the minimum wage with a living wage for all employees.

- Provide retirement benefits, including Social Security, for all employees.

- The reason to go into business would be to provide a product or service, endeavor to make a profit, and to provide a decent standard of living for employees.

- Government guaranteed financing for business expansions and startups to create jobs.

- Established enterprise zones and tax credits for job creation.

- Full employment at a living wage and benefits would allow employees to be proud of where they work.

- Lowered capital gains taxes would apply only to investments that create employment.

- Caps on salaries, wealth.

- The creation of fair taxation for all.

- Allow and protect labor unions, but not to the extent of protecting nonproductive employees.

- In concert with full employment, provide regulated child care.

- Establish a universal health care system such as Medicare for every citizen.

- Once equal economic opportunity is established under Social Capitalism, there will be a reduction in the need for legislation to try to correct bad economic policy.

- Establish that teachers, administrators, students, businesses, industries, and government get involved in public education to motivate students to be educated.

- Provide incentives to businesses to recruit high school and college students to their businesses as an incentive for them to get an education in a specific field or industry.

- Provide incentives to businesses to find ways to introduce students to the vast number and types of careers that are available.

- Require all students to have some training in business operations.

- Provide public financing of public education for every citizen through postsecondary schooling, whether college, trade schools, or other education.

- Provide that the three parties in the economy as equals would determine the proper use of natural resources, including water.

- Recognize and support the development and production of significant renewable energy resources.

- Recognize that the economic process is not complete until pollution, waste, and potential environmental damage are reclaimed, recycled, or addressed.

- Recognize and develop a dual penal system to separate hard-core criminals from nonviolent offenders.

In addition to these solutions and changes, once a true democracy is established in which government is by the majority, constitutional amendments would be considered to:

- Adopt a Social Capitalist economic system.

- Eliminate the Electoral College in favor of directly electing a president.

- Establish term limits for members of Congress.

- Adopt variations of FDR's "Economic Bill of Rights" for the working class.

- Adopt variations of Huey Long's "Share Our Wealth."

- Confirm the right of all citizens except criminals or the mentally ill to own guns.

- Ensure the rights of gays and lesbians the same as every other citizen.

- Provide that any abortion of a fetus would be by choice of the woman, but only in the first trimester except to save the life of the woman.

- Provide that capital punishment will only be in cases proven by medical or scientific means, such as DNA testing.

- Provide that the term of service for a member of the House of Representatives be four years.

- Provide that campaign financing for the presidency and Congress shall be all publicly funded.

- Establish the sanctity of voting in a democracy and ban the practice of cheating in elections with such things as voting machines that can be manipulated.

- Provide that in elections for the presidency and Congress, the top two candidates receiving the most votes during a runoff election would be placed on the ballot.

- Provide for fair, impartial local voting districts in an attempt toward equal representation.

- Provide that the right to vote will be guaranteed to every age-eligible citizen and that local government assistance must be provided to get every eligible citizen registered and able to vote in every election.

"That action is best which procures the greatest happiness for the greatest numbers."
—Francis Hutcheson

DEFINITIONS

America—The United States of America.

Capitalism—Capitalism commonly refers to an economic system in which the means of production and distribution are mostly privately owned by individual or corporate capitalists and operated for profit in a free market. (Theories of capitalism tend to pursue elimination of government regulation of property and markets.)

Capitalist—A person of great wealth (in the context of this book).

Conservative—Tending to oppose change; a person who favors traditional views and values.

Democracy—Government by the people exercised either directly or through elected representatives. A political or social unit based on democratic rule. The common people, especially as the primary source of political power. Rule by the majority. The principles of social equality and respect for the individual within a community.

Democrat—An individual supporting the interests of the people and social equality. A supporter of the Democratic Party in the United States.

Free Market—A market in which prices of goods and services are determined by the mutual consent of sellers and buyers and not persuaded by a third party (government).

Gerrymandering—A practice that attempts to establish a political advantage for a particular party or group by manipulating district boundaries to create partisan advantaged voting districts.

Greed—An excessive desire to acquire or possess, as wealth or power, beyond what one needs or deserves.

Laissez-faire—An economic environment in which transactions between private parties are free from government intervention, including regulations, taxes, tariffs, and enforced monopolies. The term means "leave it alone" in French.

Liberal—The quality of being generous and broadminded; endorsing a representative form of government; tolerant of the ideas or behavior of others.

Plutocracy—Government by the wealthy.

Privatization—The transfer of ownership of property or businesses from a government to a privately owned entity.

Progressive—Advocating progress toward better conditions, change, improvement, or reform, as opposed to wishing to maintain things as they are, especially in political matters.

Republican—An individual supporting a representative form of government in which the citizens elect representatives to government who are responsible to the citizens. A supporter of the Republican (GOP) Party in the United States. "GOP" stands for Grand Old Party.

Social Capitalism—1) An economic system characterized by recognition of the association of three parties, capitalists, labor (working class), and government, in which all parties contribute toward balanced economic development, with the right to a profit by the capitalists and the right to employment at a living wage and living benefits by the working class, with such assurances regulated by government policy. 2) An economic system regarded as being based on equality of economic opportunity between social classes.

Socialism—Socialism refers to an economic system in which property and the distribution of wealth are subject to social control invoked by the government.

Unfettered—Not controlled or limited by anyone or anything.

Unregulated—Not regulated; uncontrolled.

*"The forces in a capitalist society, if left unchecked, tend
to make the rich richer and the poor poorer."*
—Jawaharlal Nehru

I
DEMOCRACY AND CAPITALISM

The endeavor of a democracy is a government of the people, by
the people, and for the people. The democratic government of the
United States of America is hailed as the epitome of democracy.
In fact, the government of the United States is a democracy, but a
democracy of sorts, not a true democracy. A true democracy would
be a government of the people, by the people, and for the people, not
of the rich, by the rich, and for the rich. A true democracy would not
filter the national presidential election through an Electoral College
to ensure that a populist does not get elected president and spoil
everything for the rich, elite aristocracy. A true democracy would
elect a president from the majority class, the working class, the
have-nots, the noncapitalists. The true class society in the United
States is camouflaged by the use of Democrats and Republicans, or
liberals (progressives) and conservatives. In fact, the real classes are
the haves and have-nots, or capitalists and working class. The power
of the capitalists in such a democracy is gleaned from the unfettered
capitalist economic system as applied in the United States. The
working class in any democracy makes up by far the majority class,
while capitalists make up the minority class. Logically, candidates
of the minority class should never get enough votes to get elected
in a true democracy. A member of the minority capitalist class can
only be elected president if the majority class fails to get involved in
an election, or if the capitalist minority class uses extensive rhetoric,
propaganda, and deceit to gain crossover votes from the working class.

Therefore, it is quite obvious that an unfettered capitalist economic system is wrong for a democratic nation. A better economic system for a democratic nation is Social Capitalism.

In America it is taught "that all men are created equal, that they are endowed by their Creator with certain unalienable Rights, that among these are Life, Liberty, and the pursuit of Happiness" (Appendix A). It is also taught that "We the people of the United States, in Order to form a more perfect Union, establish Justice, insure domestic Tranquility, provide for the common defence, promote the general Welfare, and secure the Blessings of Liberty to ourselves and our Posterity, do ordain and establish the Constitution for the United States of America" (Appendix B). In addition, President Lincoln stated, "Four score and seven years ago our fathers brought forth on this continent, a new nation, conceived in Liberty, and dedicated to the proposition that all men are created equal…and that government of the people, by the people, for the people, shall not perish from the earth." When these ideals have been lost through the imposition of an unfettered capitalist economic system that unfairly secures power and wealth to the capitalists at the expense of the working class, alternatives must be offered in an attempt to give the working class a chance to bring about fairness in the economy before it is too late.

Millions of immigrants and refugees came to America believing in the great words that were rooted in this nation. They came with a vision of individual rights, liberty, hope, opportunity, and to seek prosperity. Upon arrival in America, many, if not most, had to have been disillusioned. They soon learned that the unfettered capitalist economic system in America was of, by, and for the capitalists. Virtually everything from the government to industry to the money supply was controlled by the capitalists under the unfettered capitalist economy. Unfettered capitalism is designed by and for the benefit of capitalists. Working class Americans under unfettered capitalism are reduced to and recognized as a commodity of labor to serve and be used up by the unfettered capitalist system. Where then was the equality, promotion of the general welfare, and the government of the people, by the people, for the people to support the pursuit of happiness? It was consumed by and for the greed of the capitalists. This greed continues today through the insistence on an American economic system of *laissez-faire*, unregulated, unfettered capitalism as part of what was proposed by Adam Smith and others. Unfettered capitalism is not an economic system of, by, and for the people, and should therefore be redressed to an economic system that serves all Americans. Unfettered capitalism is not sanctioned by law in America but is implemented and perpetrated by capitalists as a means of securing profits and wealth at all costs through greed.

In addition, in his writings on unfettered capitalism, Adam Smith wrote, "No society can surely be flourishing and happy, of which by far the greater part of the numbers are poor and miserable." Smith explicitly recognized the usefulness of public investment for projects that cannot be undertaken by the private sector—he mentions roads and education as two examples. He further writes that government has the duty of "erecting and maintaining those public institutions and those public works which may be in the highest degree advantageous to a great society." Public institutions must include those programs that would prevent the working class from being a commodity of labor through which many are poor and miserable. It seems that capitalists conveniently disregarded this part of Adam Smith's writings, probably because it would not enhance their profits. However, capitalists are emphatic about the unfettered capitalist economic system being *laissez-faire* and free from government regulation.

Capitalism originated hundreds of years ago in Europe. Absolute capitalism, which provides capitalists the right to own any and everything, including slaves, became known as unfettered capitalism.

When this unfettered capitalism was introduced in the United States, the right to own anything and everything was tempered with the adoption of the Bill of Rights to the American Constitution. However, the intent of unfettered capitalism, to allow the capitalists to control and the working class to be controlled, was retained. Some of the forms of tempering strict unfettered capitalism are a minimum wage, graduated income tax, inheritance tax, labor unions, and social programs for the less fortunate of the working class. Capitalists yet today continuously strive to eradicate these forms of tempering and desire to return to absolute unfettered capitalism and the private ownership of all methods of production and distribution without government interference. Although absolute unfettered capitalism may have been tolerated and effective in an era of totalitarianism and an uneducated working class, it has no place in a democracy of freedom and educated masses. A form of capitalism with government regulation and control over greed to provide for the welfare of the working class is much more appropriate for a democracy. Such an economic system for any democracy would be Social Capitalism as opposed to unfettered capitalism.

America has many problems that blemish the image of democracy. The use of the Electoral College is outdated. Influence peddling by capitalists and corporations raises concerns of corruption. When disgusted majority party voters refuse to vote, governments are elected by minority party voters. These governments implement special interest legislation that is not in the best interest of the working class majority. This is what has happened in America. Taxation and special interest government policy has been tailored to the special interests of the capitalist elite. True democracy must be upheld as long as America exists. There is a failure in America that is the root of most of America's problems and is potentially disastrous, but that failure is not democracy. The failure in America is the lack of an economic system that accounts for the needs of all Americans, the capitalists and the working class. The majority of Americans are the working class, who may own small businesses or be employed, but generally have only their labor to sell.

There are no simple solutions to America's problems. As with the complexities of life, solutions to issues that must provide for millions of individuals are also complex and multifaceted. Every issue interacts with other issues in a complex cause-and-effect relationship. The solution to any given issue has ramifications on other issues. For example, putting drug dealers in jail is part of the solution for illegal drug use. The rest of the solution may be revising education, welfare, job creation, the legal system, etc.

In government policy, as in logic, if the original policy or premise is morally, ethically, or socially wrong, so it will be with any attempts to make it right by future action based on that original policy or premise, regardless of its being permitted by law or custom. Simply having a declared government policy or regulation does not in itself mean that such policy or regulation is correct, fair, true, or the best alternative. It simply identifies the policy or regulation as the practice established by the government and therefore to be followed. Whenever policies or regulations are set in place, time and the ramifications of the policy or practice will determine if it is the correct policy or regulation, not the fact that it has become law or the accepted practice. Such policies and regulations must constantly be reviewed as to their impact on the people. Alternatives, if necessary, must be continually offered. It is very dangerous to a democracy when a governed people no longer seek alternatives to that which does not work, simply because it is assumed that no alternative is possible. When people will only talk about that which troubles them, without offering or demanding alternatives, those who would benefit from bad policy or regulations have won and are without competition. Such is the case with unfettered capitalism in America or any democratic nation.

An unfettered capitalist economic system is generally accepted as providing equal opportunity for all, when it clearly does not. It is false that the money of the wealthy capitalists is the fuel of an economic system. The fuel of an economy is the labor of the working class. Capitalists always use the excuse that they need limitless wealth and must not be taxed because they are the job creators. The truth is the majority of jobs are created by working class small businesses. Even more jobs are created when all the working class have jobs at living wages. Since the original concept is wrong, so are any attempts to amend the system. Since the proper economic system has not been set in place, volumes of laws and regulations have been enacted to try to make the system appear to be working, all to no avail. The economic problems will not only persist, but will get worse as attempts are made to amend them. Until the major problem of the inequality of the economic system is resolved by correction of the false premises on which it is structured, inequality will not be resolved. Many in the working class will continue to suffer as the economy fails to provide gainful employment at living wages.

Throughout history, practices have developed that have been acceptable for long periods of time. The practice being accepted by the people does not in itself make the practice right. Time and logic will prove whether most practices are right or wrong. For example, slavery was practiced for thousands of years. Slavery is acceptable, according to the Bible. Is it any wonder that slavery was an accepted practice? Further, is it any wonder that those who practiced slavery fought so vehemently to retain slavery when they had the language of the Bible on their side? Those bound and abused by slavery had no say in the matter. They were oppressed until the time came that the inhumanity of the practice of slavery was realized. Once realized by enough of the population, the process was set in motion to abolish slavery, and it was rightfully abolished. Today, slavery is generally looked upon as an atrocious practice that is a part of history that must never be repeated. Slavery was abolished in favor of the recognized moral right of all people to be free within a democracy.

Unfettered capitalism, in a similar vein to slavery, has been practiced in America since the inception of the nation. It has become the accepted economic system in America. However, an analysis of unfettered capitalism reveals fatal flaws showing that unfettered capitalism is not the correct economic system for a democratic America. In fact, unfettered capitalism provides that the working class (labor) serve to enhance the wealth of capitalists. In the capitalist business world, machinery, equipment, and technology are identified as being more valuable than labor. This is evident in the balance sheets of companies and corporations. A corporate balance sheet identifies machinery in the form of trucks and heavy equipment, etc., as assets to be depreciated as they wear out or are used up. A balance sheet identifies materials used in production as assets of the company. But where on a balance sheet is the greatest asset of labor, in the form of working class employees, reflected as an asset or equity? The answer is that employees of a corporation or business are not reflected on a balance sheet as assets or equity. In fact, employees are considered to be less than assets. Employees are to be used, used up, and discarded. If employees were treated better than assets, they could be taken care of, at least to the extent that capitalists take care of and protect their other assets. Employees would be provided at least a living wage together with a retirement plan, health care, day care, ample vacation time, etc. In today's business environment, the brains of employees are the greatest asset of a company. No business will maximize its operation without utilizing the brains of its employees to the maximum extent possible. Yet, this great asset is treated as less valuable than mechanized machinery by most companies, all in the name of more profits. Under Social Capitalism, capitalists and corporations must acknowledge their employees, provide a decent standard of living, and not treat employees as expendable.

Many believe, or have been led to believe, that there is equality through a democracy and an unfettered capitalist economic system. They believe that because democracy is supposed to provide for equality in government, that unfettered capitalism must provide for equal opportunity in the economic system. This is false. Unfettered capitalism does not provide equal opportunity to all. Democracy and unfettered capitalism are not synonymous; they are separate factors within a civilized society.

Unfettered capitalism is often appropriately referred to as vulture capitalism. Not everyone is an owner of a means of production or distribution. It isn't even true that everyone in a democracy has the opportunity to achieve the dream of a democracy. If the dream of a democracy is to be able to provide for a family, own a home, send children to college, retire comfortably, and continually strive for a better standard of living, then there isn't economic equality with unfettered capitalism.

> *Government, capitalists, and the working class are basically adversaries in the unfettered capitalism economic system. Under the proposed Social Capitalism economic system, government, capitalists, and the working class are considered three equal parties to achieve greater equality for all.*

Democracy is the governmental system in which the people, as opposed to capitalists, corporations or dictators, shall be in charge of the government. Capitalism is the economic system practiced within the democracy that provides for the private ownership of the means of production and distribution, as opposed to government ownership, as in socialism. Equality of opportunity in the capitalist economic system has never existed because of capitalism being unfettered, unregulated, and *laissez-faire*, which does not provide for equality. Unfettered capitalism provides that the capitalist class, as with the aristocracy of the past in Europe, will own the means of production and distribution. The working class, as with peasants and serfs of the past, will be provided for by selling or providing their labor to the capitalists, at the wages (if any) the capitalists wish to pay or at a minimum wage mandated by the government over the objection of capitalists. The working class will also fight the wars waged by the capitalists while the capitalists remain behind to profiteer. The unfettered capitalist system is set up to take care of the capitalists, in the hope that the capitalists will take care of all of the working class, which has not happened. However, unlike the class society of the past in Europe, those of the working class in America that are ambitious, entrepreneurial, creative, or inventive can elevate their lifestyle to the capitalist class. The vast majority of the working class in America do not or are unable to elevate their lifestyle through such means. Therefore, Social Capitalism is absolutely the economic system needed to provide an acceptable standard of living for all working class families.

There has never been a social responsibility attached to the privilege of unfettered capitalist ownership. For the less fortunate in the working class, those who are unable to find gainful employment in the unfettered capitalism system, governments generally set up social programs to attempt to ensure care and treatment, again to the objection of the greedy capitalists and their advocates. The social "safety net" programs are continually under attack by capitalists in an unfettered capitalist economic system. Capitalists continually strive for privatization and deregulation of all government agencies in their quest for obscene profits and wealth accumulation. Privatization and deregulation generally promote greater profits for already wealthy capitalists while bringing about lower wages, higher prices on goods and services, and greater risks of poverty for the working class. Privatization and deregulation also tend to open the floodgates for greed, fraud, and abuse of the working class.

Unfettered capitalism, by its very definition, is not a complete economic system. Socialism provides directly for all the people, with a degree of economic and social equality. Even communism, as absurd as it is, proposes to provide directly for all the people. Democracy, on the other hand, provides that all the people will have a voice in government as equals. Why then would a democracy have an economic system, unfettered capitalism, which does not provide economic and social equality directly for all the people? Some economists have supported the theory that unfettered capitalism should not require a social responsibility. Further, the theory assumes that society will more than benefit from the prosperity of the capitalists under unfettered capitalism. As capitalists prosper, so will the rest of society in a "trickle-down" fashion. Unfortunately, unfettered capitalism as a theory was fatally flawed without delegation of the social responsibility to provide for the working class. It was hoped that, under unfettered capitalist theory, the goodness of employers would provide for employees. The hope never materialized to the degree necessary to ensure that the working class could earn a decent living. It appears that what economists failed to factor into unfettered capitalism was the inherent greed of capitalists. Unfettered capitalism was thought to be a system that would provide equal opportunity for all, and no one bothered to ensure that it in fact would.

It is interesting to note that under unfettered capitalism, American President Ronald Reagan was actually correct that America has a trickle-down economy. Trickle-down theory is the belief that if capitalists are allowed to be wealthy, then benefits and opportunity will trickle down to the working class. Something did trickle down to the working class, but it wasn't a living wage and living benefits for all. Many have correctly determined that the trickle-down economic theory was more like a "trickle on" the working class. To wealthy Americans, President Reagan offered obscene tax cuts and wealth accumulation. To less fortunate Americans, he offered commodity cheese. There was a highway billboard in central Oklahoma that accurately reflected the Reagan presidency. It said, "Reagan takes from the needy and gives to the greedy." This is unfettered capitalism in America. There have also been statements made that Reagan's likeness should be added to Mount Rushmore. Such an addition would be an insult to the great presidents already depicted on Mount Rushmore. If any president's likeness should be added to Mount Rushmore, it should be Franklin D. Roosevelt, a true champion of the American working class. The bad policies of Reaganomics have continued and worsened to this day.

It is easy to conclude that unfettered capitalism was defined and perpetuated as being complete and correct for a democracy. This premise of unfettered capitalism has persisted without significant challenge to this day. Regardless of the origin, unfettered capitalism as a complete economic system must be put to rest in order to achieve the next step in prosperity for the working class. The next step is equal economic opportunity under a Social Capitalist economic system. Although philanthropy has benefited society to a large degree, far too many people have suffered. Are there models of Social Capitalism? Absolutely! Many European countries have economic systems of various degrees of Capitalistic Socialism that attempt to do well for all their citizens. However, it appears that the help to their working classes is disproportionate to the successes of their aristocracy.

The American Constitution is emphatic that America will be a democracy. It is, however, silent about the economic system that will perpetuate democracy. From that silence has evolved the unfettered capitalist economic system, including that proposed by the writings of Adam Smith in the 1700s. He wrote that the economy should be free of government intervention and, thereby, the economic forces could benefit everyone to the degree of his or her efforts or labor. Unfortunately, capitalists did not accept and were not required to provide for social responsibility. Therefore, government could not stay out of the economy, and no one bothered to rethink the theory to determine what the impact would be, based on the intervention of government. However, even with imperfections, capitalism has been a major contributing factor in the evolution of the greatest nation on earth. The positive aspects of capitalism must therefore be retained as we progress to a truly equitable economic system of Social Capitalism. The Bill of Rights to the United States Constitution must be expanded to provide a truly fair and equitable economic system for a democracy.

Capitalism promotes ingenuity, entrepreneurship, and innovation, none of which must ever be excluded from an equitable economic system. It is the openness of the capitalist economic system that puts the brains of humans to work to solve problems, create products, create private sector jobs, and provide for the needs of a nation. However, large corporations that are unregulated can tend to monopolize by becoming too big and working together with other large corporations to split up territories to keep out competition and increase profits. To the delight of capitalists, unfettered capitalism does not provide for social programs. Under American capitalism, capitalists greedily promote government programs and regulations that enhance their profits. But sadly, the capitalists have not stepped forward and provided for the working class with living wages and benefits. This is having it both ways. The American economic system has become the benchmark for world economies, even though the system is unbalanced and in need of correction. Enough is enough, and it is time to correct this unbalanced economic system by enacting Social Capitalism to provide for everyone in a democracy.

An unfettered capitalism economic system that provides favorably for one class of people, the capitalists, while subordinating the working class to a commodity role, is socially, morally, and ethically wrong.

A government has few resources from which to provide goods and services to the working class, other than what is extracted from the private sector through taxation. If a democratic nation had a fully employed working class under a Social Capitalist economic system, the job of government would be mostly limited to protecting the public interest and controlling capitalist greed. There would not be a drift toward Socialism to provide for the unemployed or underemployed.

It should be obvious to anyone who has studied a capitalist economic system that the single factor that drives a capitalist society is jobs at a living wage. Besides a profit motive, capitalism must provide every able-bodied member of the working class with employment opportunities. The fuel of an economic engine is working class labor. If every individual had a job at a living wage, many of the government programs in place today would not be needed. Families would be able to afford their own home or apartment, which greatly enhances the housing construction market and reduces the need for subsidized housing. The welfare system would be greatly reduced. There would be only a limited need for a food assistance program. Government Social Security programs could be strengthened. In addition, a reduction in the outflow of tax dollars for social programs would provide an increased tax base, from which necessary government programs could be adequately funded.

Businesses, in return for the wealth that is provided to them through the policies of a Social Capitalist economic system, must have a responsibility to the same employees and society that provided the opportunity for their wealth in the first place. Capitalists and corporate businesses must be taxed to the point that all the working class is either employed or their needs are met. Government must provide the policies, incentives, tax credits, or employment credits that businesses need to provide employment opportunity for all. To accomplish this, a two-partner, government and capitalist, economic relationship is not needed; the need is for a three-partner, government, capitalist, and working class relationship under Social Capitalism.

> *The essence of life should not be profits, accumulation, and greed, but rather doing the best one can while at the same time improving the living standard for employees and providing for the less fortunate.*

The democratic way must be in keeping with the essence of life. Greed is a powerful obstacle to the essence of life. As the successful become more successful, there is a tremendous drive called greed that interferes with the drive for human compassion to help others. It is very easy to shut one's eyes and shy away from the problems of others while enjoying a lifestyle that is only a dream for most people. This is especially true where the wealth was made possible through the efforts of countless employees or by inheritance. No one should be denied the right to be rewarded for his or her efforts and to enjoy his or her success. However, successful capitalists must give back to those who made their success possible. Greed and hoarding are not in keeping with an equitable democracy and economic system.

In return for the inducements that must be offered by government to businesses or for the creation of businesses that will provide for full employment, businesses must accept a responsibility. It is time for businesses to acknowledge that their employees are a major factor in their businesses. There is nothing wrong with a business making a profit for those who had the ambition and took the effort to put up the investment that created the business and the jobs for the employees. However, that profit must not be at the expense of employees but rather in concert with employees under Social Capitalism.

There can be a three-party partnership economic system, and it can lead to prosperity for all. However, it will not happen without a change in the leadership of a nation to recognize and support equal rights and opportunities for all. Capitalists and government have a responsibility to provide equal opportunity for the working class. In a capitalist democracy, as the private sector or business economy goes, so goes the nation, unless the capitalist corporations get themselves into financial trouble and scream for a government bailout. In other words, the capitalists believe that unfettered capitalism is the only economic system, unless they need a government financial bailout, which is socialistic. Nothing short of fairness will provide for an equitable economic future. In order to bring balance to a democratic economy, there must be a change from unfettered capitalism to Social Capitalism. It has been said that complaining about something does no good unless alternatives are offered. It is therefore up to the working class to get involved in their government by getting involved in the voting process to elect candidates that support the majority working class. Once a working class government is in place, the movement to eliminate unfettered capitalism and establish a Social Capitalist economic system can begin.

This book is not a "bashing the rich" undertaking. Wealthy capitalists are simply using the existing laws based on unfettered capitalism practices to amass their fortunes. When individuals are mandated to accept the rule of law in a social structure, it is the responsibility of the government of that social structure to ensure that fairness, protection, hope, and opportunity are afforded all individuals succumbing to the social structure. If the government fails to erect and maintain public institutions to fulfill such a responsibility, then certain segments of the citizenry under the government will flourish and other segments will not. Capitalists under an unfettered capitalist economic system do not believe that there is a place for government in the economy unless the government practice benefits capitalists. Capitalists believe that unfettered capitalism means that government should get out of the economy and leave the economy to its own devices, as in, let the capitalists do anything they want, including self-regulation. The fallacy of this thinking is that the greed of the capitalists has not left room for self-regulation. Therefore, it is the responsibility of the government to ensure the opportunity for social balance within the economic system of a democracy. Social balance in a civilized society is achieved through government regulation of the greed inherent under capitalism. Government regulation is an inherent part of a Social Capitalist economic system.

"Good judgment seeks balance and progress; lack of it eventually finds imbalance and frustration."
—Dwight D. Eisenhower

II
MINORITY GOVERNMENT

The primary political parties in a democracy and capitalist economic system should be divided into two camps, the haves and the have-nots. Capitalists and advocates of unfettered capitalism are the haves, and the working class is the have-nots. Haves push an agenda to maximize the wealth of capitalists, and have-nots push an agenda to help the working class enjoy a decent standard of living.

In many cases the candidates for office of a nation may not have been elected by a majority of the eligible voters as envisioned under a democracy. They have been elected by a majority of those voting, which can put a president in office that represents less than 20 percent of the people. How does this happen? If only 75 percent of the eligible population registers to vote, and only 50 percent of those registered actually vote, and the candidate is elected by 51 percent of those voting, he/she has been elected by less than 20 percent of the population of eligible voters. For example:

Total eligible to vote	180,000,000
Registered voters (75 percent)	135,000,000
Registered voters who vote (50 percent)	67,500,000
Official elected by 51 percent	34,425,000
(34,425,000 is less than 20 percent of 180,000,000)	

Can the above example actually happen? Absolutely! Should it ever happen? Never! This is not the intended democratic way! It's no wonder that a democracy has so many problems when the whole population does not vote.

Democracy is defined as rule by the majority, the common people, especially as the primary source of political power. The majority in a democracy is the working class. Therefore, if all of the working class eligible to vote actually voted and voted for their own interests, they would elect a majority working class government. The unfettered capitalists and advocates of unfettered capitalist ideals as represented by the haves are the minority party. In order to have a minority party government, the minority party must revert to trickery, misinformation, cheating, etc., to entice working class voters to switch their votes to the other side. Techniques used to entice majority class voters to switch their votes to the other side are the use of voting machines that can be manipulated and cannot be manually verified, playing up single issues such as gun control, gay rights, religion, gerrymandering of state electoral districts, voter suppression, purging minority voters from voter rolls, phantom votes, votes not counted, and any other tactics they can get away with. In addition, capitalists systematically take ownership of all the media outlets they can to prevent reporting on progressive ideals. They will even go so far as to spin progressive ideals to conservative leanings. However, if the working class voters who are coerced into voting with capitalists would follow-up to see exactly what legislation the capitalists support, it would become clear that capitalists support capitalist ideals to enhance the wealth of capitalists and not to improve the standard of living for the working class. Working class voters have to be made aware that these tactics are utilized simply to get enough votes to accomplish a minority government. Once elected, the minority government works only to enhance the wealth of capitalists at the expense of the working class. It appears that greedy capitalists want total control of government and the vote. Such control could prevent the capitalist minority class from ever being defeated in future elections or ever relinquishing the government to a democracy.

> *"The marvel of all history is the patience with which men and women submit to burdens unnecessarily laid upon them by their governments."*
> —William E. Borah

All it takes for the eligible voting public to ensure that future generations will not have to be subjected to the tainted policies of a minority (capitalist) government is to register to vote and then vote. Democracy does not need a minority government. It needs a government of all the people to provide for all the people as intended in a democracy. It needs a government that will recognize that the unfettered capitalist economic system does not provide for everyone equally. Unfettered capitalism will continue to be perpetuated in a democracy by the millions who fail to register to vote or actually vote. It is time for every eligible citizen in a democracy to register and vote.

Capitalists and advocates of capitalist ideals believe in one thing above all else. They believe in unfettered capitalism and profits at all costs. They do not believe in government regulations to ensure fairness and safety for the working class. They believe that all government regulations over the economy should be eliminated so that they would have a free reign in the marketplace, with no minimum wage, no employee benefits, no environmental regulations, no taxes, no universal health care, no Social Security, and no government programs except those programs that provide for capitalist and corporate subsidies. In addition, they believe that it should be perfectly permissible to move business out of a country to achieve cheaper labor and thus greater profits at the expense of working class jobs. In other words, capitalists prefer a "survival of the fittest" society rather than a civilized society, so they may expand their greed to all quarters. These actions are not only antidemocratic but also unpatriotic.

Plutocracy is defined as government by the wealthy capitalists and corporations. Plutocracy has been present in America for many years, which renders democracy to a figure of speech and not a practical application. Plutocratic ideals have generally been upheld by the United States Supreme Court. Support for those with money and wealth over working class citizens in the political arena greatly weakens a democracy. If America is to be the model democracy for other nations of the world to look up to and emulate, then money and wealth must not be the focus for attaining political office. Plutocracy reinforces unfettered capitalism and greed. Plutocracy, unfettered capitalism, and greed must be eliminated in favor of Social Capitalism.

A democracy will not survive with a government controlled by greedy capitalists and their advocates. It has been said that great nations eventually are destroyed not by enemies from outside the country, but rather from within. This destruction from within is generally caused by a combination of greed, lust for power, and failure of the government to address the needs of the majority working class citizens. Some believe that in America, the process has already begun. The massive accumulation of wealth by capitalists, sheltering the wealth in banks overseas or offshore, and the starting of a war over oil profits, are evidence to support such statements. The Great Depression took America to the brink of disaster, but, through democratic leadership, America was restored to an assimilation of democracy. The Great Depression was brought on by unfettered capitalists' greed, speculation, and leveraging beyond their means with total disregard for the working class. The same greed brought on the savings-and-loan bailout and is again surfacing with mortgage speculation and multiple bank failures. This unfettered capitalist greed will continue as long as unfettered capitalism is the economic policy in America. Significant practices have already been set in place to prevent the working class from gaining control of the federal government. Examples are talk shows and television networks that side with capitalists to present capitalist/corporate spin of daily news, pressuring candidates for office to pledge not to raise taxes, and election campaigns where only the wealthiest can afford to run for office.

Capitalists' being a minority in America requires them to use every trick in the book to entice the working class to vote with the capitalists in order to gain enough votes to take control of the government. Capitalist propaganda generally lends in the direction of telling them what they (the working class) want to hear so the capitalists can get their votes, but once they get elected, the capitalists give them privatization, deregulation, and tax cuts with wealth accumulation for the rich. To accomplish this, they have learned that many of the working class are very passionate on certain national issues, such as gun control, gay rights, and religion. The capitalists and advocates use this passion to structure their campaigns to draw some of the working class to vote with capitalists. One of the cheapest tricks is to get the working class to believe that the rich create jobs with tax cut money when the reality is that the money is being stockpiled in offshore or overseas banks. The truth is that the working class voters who vote with capitalists are voting against their own interests. When the capitalists get into power, they support the capitalist wealth accumulation agenda and not an agenda to enhance the living standard of the working class. Under capitalist minority administrations, the living standard of the working class declines, taxes on the wealthy are cut, and unions are attacked. Eventually, if capitalist minority administrations continue, the nation will be so far in debt due to tax cuts for the wealthy that the currency will have to be significantly devalued. Inflation will erode savings and retirements to the point where what was thought to be a comfortable retirement for the working class is no longer there. To stop this slide into destruction, the working class must vote their interests by voting for the working class to hold national and state offices. Working class voters should not be taken in by the rhetoric and propaganda of the minority class. It has been said many times that democracy is not a spectator sport. Democracy only works if every qualified citizen gets involved and votes his or her interests in all elections.

Throughout history, civilizations that have been dominated by the wealthy have resulted in uprisings of the workers once conditions became intolerable. In America, conditions for most are not yet that intolerable. America's problems can be corrected by peaceful means. We must elect a democratic government of the working class. The unfettered capitalist economic system must be replaced with the adoption of the Social Capitalist economic system. Such a movement must begin by encouraging every eligible American to vote his or her best interest as a working class American or a capitalist. Once a true democratic government of the majority is attained, then a move to abolish unfettered *laissez-faire* capitalism and adopt Social Capitalism can begin.

"Capital is only the fruit of labor, and could never have existed if labor had not first existed."
—Abraham Lincoln

III
SOCIAL CAPITALISM

Providing a responsible Social Capitalist economic system is the next natural step to be taken in the quest for "life, liberty, and the pursuit of happiness" for everyone in a democracy. The flaw in unfettered capitalism is the fact that the wealthy elite capitalists have the privilege of capital accumulation and private ownership of the means of production and distribution, but are allowed to disregard the social responsibility that must go with it. In other words, if capitalists are afforded the privileges of private capital accumulation and ownership, they must also be held to the social responsibility of providing adequately for the working class. Capitalists are afforded the privilege of private accumulation, which would otherwise be held by the government, as in socialism. If the government held the means of production and distribution publicly, the government through job creation or government programs would also ensure the welfare of the entire population. The responsibility for providing for the population must therefore remain assigned to those in control of the means of production and distribution. With socialism, the government owns the means of production and distribution and therefore would provide for the population. With unfettered capitalism as practiced today, capitalists have been afforded the role of government as owners, but have not taken the responsibility to provide for the working class. The major failure of unfettered capitalist theory is not requiring the capitalists to take responsibility for providing for the needs of the working class. This failure is in keeping with the insistence by capitalists that the government stay out of the economy, as in "unfettered." Providing for the working class has been relegated to the government, which has no means except taxation with which to provide for the needs of the working class.

Social Capitalism is not a new concept. It has been around for years in European countries under differing names. It has also been identified and discussed in America off and on for years in different concepts. An example would be the concepts brought out by Senator Huey Long in 1934 in his plan to "Share Our Wealth." Another example is from Franklin Delano Roosevelt in 1944 when he proposed a "Second Bill of Rights" or "Economic Bill of Rights." Social Capitalism is the recognition that under the freedom proposed by a democracy, the marvelous benefits of the economic system should not be reserved primarily for the wealthy, elite capitalists and their advocates. A democratic economy should benefit the entire population of a democracy by providing all the people with the hope, opportunity, and prosperity that are the product of a democratic nation. This is not accomplished with *laissez-faire* unfettered capitalism, which unfairly benefits the wealthy capitalists over the working class. It is accomplished by regulating and controlling capitalist greed through Social Capitalism.

Capitalism is the part of the system that provides that the capitalists will own the means of production and distribution. It is also the part that inspires the human mind to build the better mouse trap and to invent computers. The human mind must be free and never restrained from expanding the interests of humanity. In the case of America, capitalism has brought America to what it is today. This inspiration must not be hindered in the future, but must be expanded to involve all Americans, as would be accomplished with a Social Capitalist economic system.

The "Social" in Social Capitalism is the part of the economic system that recognizes that in a civilized society there must be an association or partnership between capitalists, labor (working class), and government. All parties must contribute toward balanced economic development. Capitalists must have the right to earn profits. The noncapitalist working class must have the right to employment at a living wage and living benefits. Government must provide assurances through regulation and policy. Social Capitalism recognizes a social system regarded as being based on equality of economic opportunity between social classes to mesh with the equity proposed in a democracy.

> *"All that is necessary for the triumph of evil is that good men do nothing."*
> —Edmund Burke

The adoption of Social Capitalism would bring about change. These changes would be to the benefit of all and the detriment of none. The labor or working class would enjoy a higher standard of living and the ability to enjoy all that life has to offer. The capitalists would not be allowed to greedily accumulate obscene wealth and would have a social responsibility in return for the benefits of a capitalist component in the economy. This would result in a balanced economy. There must be a capitalist component in order to promote and enhance entrepreneurship and invention. There must also be a social responsibility to provide adequately for the working class. Social Capitalism would be based on the principles of social equality and respect for the individual within a community. Following in this chapter are some of the benefits that would result from the adoption of Social Capitalism.

Social Capitalism in a civilized society recognizes that with the capitalist privilege of private ownership of the means of production and distribution goes the social responsibility to ensure that all able-bodied working class people are employed at a living wage and benefits. Government must facilitate full employment with incentives to the private sector. Only with the adoption of Social Capitalism will a democratic nation reach its full potential as an equitable democracy. Greater equality in the economy will only be achieved by electing candidates with integrity to government offices.

"No democracy can long survive which does not accept as fundamental to its very existence the recognition of the rights of minorities."

—Franklin D. Roosevelt

1. Democracy

Democracy is defined as rule by the majority, the common people, especially as the primary source of political power and the principles of social equality, and respect for the individual within a community. If democracy is rule by the majority, the common people (working class), why isn't America ruled by the working class? The answer goes back to the Constitution. The framers of the Constitution, whether intentionally or by mistake, chose not to require all eligible Americans to vote in elections. Whether it was a negotiated decision or a decision based on the freedom of choice as to vote or not to vote, nevertheless, voting was not mandated. The question then becomes, how can there be rule by the majority if not every eligible voter votes? The answer then becomes, you don't have rule by the majority, but rather by a majority of voters in a best-case scenario, given only two candidates. If there are three or more candidates, it could result in rule by less than a majority of those voting. Without a rule that all eligible voters are required to vote, it can and does leave a minority group such as capitalists and their advocates to attempt to suppress the majority from voting so that the minority capitalist class can win and thus govern.

"If there's been class warfare in this country, my class won."

—Warren Buffett

When a nation does not have a declared economic policy that provides for equal opportunity, there is no standard for the people to use in determining if politicians are doing their job. Without a declared economic policy, influential political or private sector factions entice politicians to enact legislation to favor their special interests at the expense of the working class. Social Capitalism would provide the declared economic policy to hold politicians accountable.

Life is about change. Even the framers of the Constitution of the United States of America provided for constitutional changes to address future needs of the nation. However, capitalists and conservatives do not want change unless the change would enhance their control over the nation and its wealth. Real change in America should be to enhance the lives of millions of the working class by abolishing unfettered capitalism and adopting Social Capitalism.

> *"Man is a political animal."*
> —Aristotle

Democracy is supposed to offer a fair opportunity for all through a government that is based on principles of social equality. However, when there is no declared economic policy to support social equality, tremendous pressure is placed on politicians to function other than in the public interest. Crime in the streets, an increasing number of people in poverty, increased numbers of unemployed, homelessness, career politicians, unbalanced taxation, lack of affordable health care, racism, lack of direction for the children, and a public education system that is targeted for privatization are not the democratic way. This is ample proof that politicians will function in other than the best interest of the majority of the people. There are those in government that will tell the people that there are no solutions to economic problems, and they are doing the best they can. There are others that will expound that there are no problems, that democracy is the greatest society on earth, and how dare anyone say otherwise. These individuals are catering to special interests and do not know how or what to change, or have no desire to resolve a nation's problems because they or those they support are profiting immensely from the current unfettered capitalist economic system.

The first step toward legislating a Social Capitalist economic system for a democracy is to establish government by the majority working class. To accomplish a majority government and in order to implement a true democracy and a Social Capitalist economic system, all of the working class must register to vote and then vote their interests in all elections. Once a majority government is in place, the move to a Social Capitalist economic system can begin.

There must be a plan that will keep a democracy on the cutting edge of a changing world. What is needed to achieve a plan for the future is progressive, logical, business-oriented leadership, and a rethinking of the shortcomings of the unfettered capitalist economic system. It is up to the people, the voters, and the working class to vote to provide the leadership that is necessary to guide democracy into the future.

A big step in providing change in a democracy is to elect a statesman or stateswoman president. However, simply electing a statesman/ stateswoman president, with the business sense, logical reasoning ability, and integrity that is needed, is not enough. Members of Congress must also have similar attributes. There must be an ingrained desire in both branches of government to do what is best for the majority of the people. This requires the voters to screen political candidates carefully. There may be members of Congress now who would gladly and truthfully sign on to such a direction if it would result in what is best for the majority. The voters must ensure that such members are retained and the rest replaced. It is a sad day in the history of a democracy when members of Congress who would support change choose not to seek reelection rather than be a party to an out-of-control government. They and others like them are to be applauded and should be persuaded to serve because of their convictions.

> *True respect for a person in a position requiring leadership is not commanded, it is earned, and it is abhorrently difficult to respect the person if he/she has not earned respect by addressing the needs of the majority.*

The working class majority must insist that enough is enough. It is time for the working class to take control of the government by voting as intended in a true democracy. They must "employ" a president and Congress that will support the working class and provide the leadership that the majority deserves.

In a democracy the working class must elect a president, Congress, and state governments that will provide leadership for everyone in the nation, not just those voting. This can only be done if the majority votes candidates into office that will provide sound business leadership. Again, the whole issue is right versus wrong. It is wrong to abuse a political office for personal interests and the prosperity of the capitalists, rather than providing for the needs of the majority working class. It is wrong to subject more people to suffering rather than pursuing actions that will create jobs and restore the economy to its great potential. In short, if the primary objective is to deal with world leaders and foreign countries, elect an aristocrat for president. However, if the primary objective is that which it should be, namely, to manage the affairs of a democratic people and put them to work, elect a president who has the business sense and integrity to do just that.

A person does not have to be a genius and should not have to be wealthy to become a leader, particularly a president, member of

Congress, or a member of state government. He or she must, however, be intellectually able to reason and resolve problems to a logical conclusion and enact laws accordingly. He or she must be a statesman or stateswoman able to identify his or her goals and work to achieve them rather than letting personal or special interests interfere. He or she must be willing and able to commit to supporting the majority working class in a democracy.

"Public office is a public trust."
—W. C. Hudson

"The world's great men have not commonly been great scholars, nor great scholars great men."
—Dr. Oliver Wendell Holmes

2. Voting

Many in a democracy have the intelligence and ability to contribute to the management of the affairs of a nation by serving in Congress and state governments. However, they are not going to enter an arena when the deck is stacked against them through rule by the capitalist wealthy and incumbency. These patriotic people would gladly give of their time to help the country, but their integrity will not allow them to participate in a charade political system imposed by the wealthy and that protects the incumbent and the incumbent's interests. They will not participate in a government in which the president, members of Congress, and members of state governments are engaged in adversarial infighting day after day. They would, however, participate in a government and economic system that is logical and fair under Social Capitalism. Working class citizens must begin by voting into office those who would be of the utmost integrity, would use logical reasoning to develop sound business decisions under Social Capitalism, and would make a democratic government into what it should always be: statesmanlike.

In the United States of America, one need not have voted to complain or comment on the operating of the government or any particular elected official. It is often the people who do not vote who in turn are the biggest critics of the way their government is being handled. There has always been a traditional work ethic in America: everything that is achieved is earned. In turn, hard work can earn the way to a better life. Why should this ethic not be the same when it comes to voting for those who would make the laws? In a democracy an individual earns the right to comment or complain by first voting.

It is not surprising that America as a nation is in the spot it is in today. It is, in fact, logical to conclude that if the entire political noncapitalist majority does not vote while the political capitalist minority does, a minority or, at best, a split government will result. It is no wonder that qualified candidates who wish to represent the political majority do not choose to run for office when many of the majority party will not take the time to vote. It is no wonder that a political minority would take advantage of such a situation to enhance their own interests by pursuing election to an office that otherwise would be unattainable. Blame cannot be placed on those politicians who are elected by a political minority and then serve that minority, for that has become the American way. Blame can, however, be placed on politicians who would put their own interests ahead of the interests of the people. Though one is elected by a political minority, it is a lack of integrity and statesmanship or stateswomanship that casts a vote against the political majority, however rationalized.

In a democracy many people choose not to get involved in the process that sends politicians to office and elects a president. A major factor for nonparticipation by voters is that it is perceived that many politicians act in their own interest, with or without input from the voters. Thus, many people see no reason to participate by voting, which is the ultimate voice of the people in a democratic nation. The statement is continually heard that individuals do not vote because their "one" vote won't make a difference anyway. Individuals believe whoever is going to be elected will be elected whether "I" vote or not, and what will be will be. The statement is also made that there isn't one candidate running that is worth voting for, and since I can't change that, why vote?

The people who offer these excuses for not voting are partially correct. Seldom does one vote make the difference between winning and losing an election. At times the choices are a matter of picking the lesser of two evils. However, there is far more to the privilege of voting than merely electing an individual to office. A working class voter that doesn't vote his or her own interests is effectively casting a vote for the other side and against his or her own interests. This is why the capitalists make such an effort to discourage working class voters who would vote their own interests from voting. It is also why the capitalists use propaganda, misinformation, and single issues to get working class voters to vote against their own interests. There is a saying that "actions speak louder than words." All voters should heed this saying when it comes to politicians. Politicians, especially capitalist/corporate ones, that want working class votes, will say anything to try and persuade the working class to vote for them. The working class must look at the actions of politicians in office to determine if their political promises to the working class are actually carried out. It will become obvious that not only are the political promises to the working class not carried out, capitalist/corporate politicians will actually legislate against the working class nearly every time.

> *"You can fool some of the people all of the time, and all of the people some of the time, but you cannot fool all of the people all of the time."*
> —Abraham Lincoln

Numbers count, and those who vote will have done as much to bring about change in a democracy as those for whom they vote. Those who have not chosen to vote in the past, for whatever reason, must become involved in the opportunity to support an alternative to politics as usual. They have the opportunity to support a democracy as it was intended to be, not the way it has evolved where criminals walk the streets, law-abiding citizens are hostages in their homes, rights are continually being rescinded, career politicians dominate government, businesses have no incentive to provide jobs, private funds derived from tax cuts for the wealthy are pumped into the stock market or tax havens instead of job creation, health care and insurance costs are no longer affordable, many children go to bed hungry and are brought up without direction, homelessness increases, and education, race relations, and the elderly continue to suffer. A change to Social Capitalism can make a huge difference.

Voters should use logic as the basis for election decisions in a democracy of the majority. Without logical decisions, reasoning can become politically rationalized, resulting in solutions that do not represent the will of the people. Rationalizing solutions to problems is not new. It has evolved as the basis for politics and politicians.

What is logic or critical reasoning?

Logic may be defined as the science that evaluates arguments. All of us encounter arguments in our day-to-day experience. We read them in books and newspapers, hear them on television, and formulate them when communicating with friends and associates. The aim of logic is to develop a system of methods and principles that we may use as criteria for evaluating the arguments of others and as guides in constructing arguments of our own.

An argument, as it is used in logic, is a group of statements, one of which (the conclusion) is claimed to follow from the other or others (the premises). All arguments may be placed in one of two basic groups: those in which the conclusion really does follow from the premises, and those in which it does not, even though it is claimed to. The former are said to be good arguments, the latter bad arguments. The purpose of logic, as the science that evaluates arguments, is thus to develop methods and techniques that allow us to distinguish good arguments from bad.

—Patrick J. Hurley

A basic premise of democracy is that the people think for themselves, develop reasonable (logical) conclusions by critical thinking, and then exercise their conclusions by voting for the candidates that come closest to the same conclusions. Unfortunately, in today's governments, there are far too many elected officials who would have the people believe that their conclusions are logical, when in fact they are not.

Abraham Lincoln once pointed this out to an opponent during a debate. Apparently, the opponent kept drawing false conclusions because the premises of his arguments were repeatedly false. Of course, he was also trying to get the audience to believe his false conclusions to gain politically. Finally, Mr. Lincoln could take no more and decided to expose the error in his opponent's message. He asked his opponent to look at a dog that had found its way into the crowd. While viewing the dog, Mr. Lincoln asked his opponent, if he called the dog's tail a leg, how many legs would the dog have? His opponent immediately replied, "Five!" No, Mr. Lincoln stated; you see, it doesn't matter what you call the dog's tail—you can plainly see that it is still a tail, and therefore the dog only has four legs.

This practice of trying to get the public to believe something that is not true is quite common. Politicians are doing it all the time in hopes that enough voters will believe them so they may get elected and reelected. The lesson to be learned here is that someone making a statement and claiming it is true does not in itself make the statement true. The premises from which the statement is drawn must also be true in order for the statement to be true. This is where politicians gain an advantage over the public. Many political statements, laws, and regulations are drawn from premises that are false or have not been proven, making it difficult for the public not to draw the same conclusion. However, by applying logic, the statement, in reality, can many times be shown to be true or false.

In a true democracy, once a declaration of equality in economic opportunity is established under a Social Capitalist economic system, a reduction in the need for legislation will follow. If the correct policy is in place, there is no need to continually offer legislation to try to make bad policy seem right. In conjunction with correcting policy, it would be mutually beneficial to the public and to the government to establish an automatic sunset (review every ten years) on all legislation. This would include reviewing all legislation on the books to ensure the intended purpose is still proper and in the public interest. Many laws, regulations, and policies are merely theories when enacted, and must be proven over time. In addition, they must be revisited to ensure that the original intent is being upheld.

In drafting and executing legislation into law, the primary concern must be right versus wrong for the majority, using logical reasoning and integrity. It is wrong to enact laws that are in the special interest of a minority and against the majority. Any particular issue presented for legislative action to resolve a problem can provide any of several possible solutions. It all depends on the intent of those drafting the legislation. That intent must be in the interest of the majority. Since every problem has many possible solutions, the intent of the legislation must be carefully scrutinized by those of the utmost integrity. This emphasizes the importance of voting for candidates who have the utmost integrity.

2.1   Two-Party Political System

In a democracy and unfettered capitalist economic system, the two social classes, whether officially recognized or not, are the capitalists and labor (the working class). The working class is the majority and capitalists are the minority. Every eligible voter in such a democracy is either a capitalist or a member of the working class. However, this does not mean that all capitalists must vote for the minority and all of the working class must vote for the majority. That is the essence of a democracy that is designated a classless society: voters can vote for anyone they choose. However, the significance is that if elected, the capitalist minority class will generally pursue enhancement of the profits and wealth of capitalists at the expense of a decent living standard for the working class.

A two-party political system evolves because of the "haves" and "have-nots," capitalists and working class, or so-called conservatives and liberals or progressives. In America, the political system has evolved to become one political party that believes that unfettered capitalism is sacred and another party that has compassion for the working class, minorities, and the less fortunate. Of course capitalist beliefs and compassion exist in both parties, but the principal division is unfettered capitalism at all costs versus fairness, equality, and compassion for all. Since there can't be two correct views, which party, then, upholds the correct viewpoint? Neither party is entirely right or entirely wrong. It is the unfettered capitalist system, as explained earlier, that is at fault. An economic system based on the acceptance of Social Capitalism would result in greater economic social equality. Under Social Capitalism, capitalism can be supported because of the social responsibility that would go with it, and the working class is provided for with a reduced need for federal social programs. A major difference under a Social Capitalist economic system would be control of the government by the working class in order to control the inevitable quest for greed by capitalists.

Two political parties in a democracy, when selecting candidates and party positions or platforms, will negotiate, compromise, and adjust to the will of the party. This continues from the very beginning of the election process to the very end. This process results in one candidate finally being selected to represent the party and its platform on the ballot. Former candidates support the selected candidate in hopes of a party victory at the polls. The question becomes, why does such negotiating, compromising, and adjusting stop once the election is over? Why shouldn't the same procedure continue between parties once the candidates are seated? In a democracy, aren't the elected representatives the servants of all the people? The economic separation between the capitalists and working class results in a political system that deviates from the path of statesmanship and stateswomanship, and the time has come for it to be corrected with a Social Capitalist economic system. Once elected, the call must be to act as statesmen/women, not partisan politicians.

As long as an unfettered capitalist system is perpetuated without responsibility to provide for the needs of the working class, social program spending is totally justified. Correction of an economic system to Social Capitalism and the related controls over capitalist greed will reduce the need for some social programs. With controls over capitalist greed in place, harmony would be more likely toward a statesmanlike government.

An adversarial relationship between the two major political parties in a democracy greatly affects the inner structure of the government. Party dominance, seniority, and career politicians result in a legislative process that is controlled by those who have achieved political power within the system. Much of the legislation that would address the needs of the public never materializes because of the power held by a dominant few, especially in Congress. Government under Social Capitalism must be restructured to minimize the power and influence of the few. Additionally, laws that should be in place to protect the interests and standard of living of the working class should be constitutional amendments in order to remove them from partisan politics. Simple laws that would enhance the standard of living of the working class can be passed into law under a majority party administration, but when a minority party administration gains power, the same laws can be rescinded.

Capitalist Minority Party

The minority party, once elected, will maximize their effort to enhance the wealth of the capitalists and do little or nothing to enhance the standard of living of the working class, even for those that voted for the minority party. Many of the working class have been coerced through capitalist propaganda on a single issue to vote for the minority party. These individuals should begin to assess their future without medical insurance, Social Security, Medicare, Medicaid, and unions, and with higher taxes, lower wages, and fewer benefits. Once in office, capitalists do not support the enhancement of the standard of living for the working class regardless of the rhetoric and propaganda expounded to gain votes for the minority party candidates. In addition, with privatization and deregulation, the working class should prepare for significant changes if the minority party is elected, such as the elimination of the minimum wage, all federal and possibly state highways becoming toll roads, the elimination of Social Security and Medicare, the elimination of all social programs and assistance, the privatization of schools, privatization of correctional facilities, privatization of air traffic control, and privatization of all government inspection services, to mention a few of the possible changes. All the deregulation and privatization is part of the profiteering at all costs desired by the capitalists under unfettered capitalism. However, don't be surprised if capitalists try to rationalize the deregulation and privatization of government services under the pretense that government is inefficient and costly and the private sector can do it better. It won't be better when working class people are dying of food poisoning or airplane crashes or malnutrition, all in the name of capitalist profits. A better course of action is to support a democracy, majority government, and Social Capitalism.

In America, according to the US Census Bureau, in 2010 the four hundred richest Americans had an increase in their wealth of 54 percent while the wealth of the median middle-class family declined by 35 percent. Tax cuts for the superrich have contributed dramatically to this obscene wealth accumulation. The tax cuts, especially the capital gains tax cut to 15 percent, which was supposed to encourage job creation, went not to job creation but to the wealth accumulation of the rich. The capital gains tax cut came at a time when it was determined that the investment of big money yielded a far greater return than it did creating jobs. Once again the taxpayers were misled and the rich got richer and will continue to get richer until the capital gains tax at 15 percent is only allowed for job-creating investment. Social Capitalism would include regulation over wealth accumulation, create fair taxation, especially of the capitalists, and develop a policy of full employment.

The minority party is a self-proclaimed conservative party, following in the tradition of capitalism. However, in recent minority party administrations in America such as the Reagan administration and George W. Bush administration, the so-called conservatives have spent the country into obscene debt well beyond anything witnessed in previous

Democratic so-called liberal administrations. The obscene debt would not be there if capitalists had paid their share of taxes under Social Capitalism to offset the spending.

Generally, American economists support unfettered capitalism. Most economists declare that the primary reason to go into business is to make a profit. This is unfettered capitalism at its worst, but it justifies capitalists in their quest to be able to hoard their profits without providing for the working class and without having to pay their fair share of taxes. This is another reason that America needs Social Capitalism. Social Capitalism would establish that the reasons to go into business are, first, to provide a product or service desired or needed by Americans; second, to endeavor to make a profit in providing the product or service; and third, to provide a decent standard of living for the employees who make the product or service and profit possible. Any business that can't achieve these three objectives does not deserve to be in business.

<u>Working Class Majority Party</u>

The majority party is the working class. Some benevolent capitalists also vote with the majority party. The majority party should be in control of the government in both the presidency and in both houses of Congress in a democracy. That is, the majority party could be in control of the government if all the working class voted and voted their own interests as the working class and did not get enticed by the propaganda of the capitalists to cast a perceived single-issue vote.

The majority party is labeled as "liberal" or "progressive," tax and spend. Capitalists and sympathizers support this label as if it were a bad thing. In fact, because of an unfettered capitalist economic system, it is exactly the correct action to be taken by the majority party that supports the working class. Fair taxing of the wealthy and spending on the needy is proper policy. Being labeled "liberal" or "progressive" is in keeping with the fact that capitalists do not and will not provide for the well-being of the working class. With capitalists hoarding their profits, striving to cut the taxes on the wealthy, sheltering their profits in offshore banks to avoid taxes, refusing to support an increased minimum wage to a living wage, constantly eroding employee benefits, hindering the ability of the working class to register to vote, and so on, being a liberal or progressive of the majority party is an honor.

Independents

Under the premise that there are only capitalists and the working class in a democracy and unfettered capitalist economic system, there are no strictly independent candidates. There can only be independent capitalists or independent working class candidates. Independent capitalists are sympathetic to the capitalist minority party and wealth accumulation, while independent working class candidates are sympathetic to the working class majority party. Most candidates that declare they are independent do so because they were unsuccessful in securing the party endorsement or because they want to be a spoiler in the election. It is similar with other proposed political parties.

2.2 Statesmen/Stateswomen

Politicians who would put their own interests aside for the people in a nonpartisan manner are called statesmen and stateswomen. A statesman/woman is one who will decide in the interests and well-being of the majority. The Constitution fully intended that the government would function in a statesmanlike manner. Unfortunately, the economic system that would perpetuate a statesmanlike democracy in a manner to provide equality in economic opportunity never materialized. The lack of a declared economic policy taints a capitalist economic system and results in the evolution of a partisan two-party political system. A two-party system that pits the "haves" against the "have-nots," capitalists against the working class, prevents the conduct of government in a statesmanlike manner.

> *The first rule for anyone elected to represent the interests of a body of people is to "forego special interests in favor of the interest of the majority."*

Honesty and integrity, in addition to communication, negotiation, and compromise, are the standards that put statesmen/stateswomen above politicians in providing for the interests of all the people. Therefore, it is the voters who must insist that elected officials provide service to the public in a statesmanlike manner. The filtering of ideas, problems, and solutions results in purity. The brains of elected officials are the filters through which the public interest is supposed to be refined and made into law. Such laws need to be as pure as possible, to be free of impurities and special interests that would render them unworkable.

> *"A politician thinks of the next election; a statesman, of the next generation."*
> —James Freeman Clarke

Some candidates with statesmanlike qualities are already in government. While trying to make a difference, they are thwarted by partisan party politics. If given the opportunity to work with leadership that is also statesmanlike, they will make a difference. These are people who will do the job that is required, and not for personal gain. Unfortunately, some who would serve the people in a statesmanlike manner have found the system swamped in partisan politics to the point that they have chosen not to seek election or reelection. There are others who will not even run with such a tainted system in place. These are exactly the type of people who are needed, but the system shuts them out from doing what is right. Voters must find these candidates and encourage them to seek office as representatives of the people. With a Social Capitalist economic system, they must be persuaded to join those statesmen/women already in the government to correct the inequitable policies that have resulted in partisan government.

"He serves his party best who serves his country best."
—Rutherford B. Hayes

Politicians are the elected representatives of the people. A Social Capitalist economic system must start with the selection of representatives to government who understand and support such an effort. Politicians who seek office to promote themselves or special interests must be replaced with statesmen/women representatives who will support what is right for the majority. This can happen only if the people want it to happen and follow through by electing statesmen/women with integrity to office. Elected officials with integrity are more open to achieve changes that would be beneficial to all.

It is just as important to have staff and aides in government that think and reason logically as it is to have such attributes in the president or members of Congress. As elected officials come and go, the staffs and aides remain on many committees, and they can retain a singular viewpoint. This makes it very difficult to effect change unless logic is injected at some point. The working class must insist that their elected representatives require that logic and statesmanship or stateswomanship be present and utilized throughout government employees and staff. It does little good to have integrity and logic in the leader if those around him or her do not have the same attributes. When inadequate staff is available to an elected official because of a lack of funding, reliance is placed on that staff already in place. Without logical reasoning abilities to determine the best interests of the public, an elected official is at the mercy of such staff. If the staff is not of the utmost integrity, they may be influenced by special interests and power to the detriment of the interests of the public.

2.3 Voter Registration

One of the most sacred acts in a democracy is the responsibility and duty to vote. The Constitution stipulates that the right of citizens of the United States to vote shall not be denied or abridged by the United States or by any State on account of race, color, or previous condition of servitude...on account of age...account of sex, or...failure to pay any poll tax or other tax. But even with these constitutional guarantees, there are factions within the minority party that choose to put impediments in place to discourage working class citizens from voting. Once again, if fewer of the majority working class vote, it is easier for the capitalist minority party candidates to get enough votes to be elected. This practice of impeding voters is undemocratic and unpatriotic. In reality, if the minority party claim to be the patriotic party, they would be doing everything in their power to simplify and assist all citizens to register to vote and then vote in every election as intended in a true democracy. Under Social Capitalism the people must insist that simplified voter registration and the right to vote be mandated.

Democratic policy must include that every eligible citizen should become a registered voter and then exercise that right to vote in every election, if it is to be a true democracy. Registering to vote and then voting is the means by which all citizens will have their voices heard. It is the means by which the government can truly be representative of the majority in a democracy. It is the means by which favoritism or biases toward specific groups are eliminated, or at least those responsible can be held accountable. It is the means by which the public interest and the interests of the people are upheld through the actions of their government.

There is no magic or mystery involved in registering to vote and then voting. Every voting age citizen who is not registered must contact his or her local government to find out exactly how to register in his or her area. It is amazing to see the number of citizens who do not register or vote because it is too much bother. Anyone who is bound and determined not to vote cannot be forced to do so, for that is the American way. However, in a true democracy every citizen should be encouraged to vote. Those who are registered to vote should provide every assistance and encouragement to those around them to get involved in the voting process for the sake of future generations. However, due to the division between capitalists and the working class under unfettered capitalism, some do not want everyone to be registered to vote.

In a democracy, people can complain about government even if they are not involved in the government by voting. It takes courage, commitment, vision, and ambition to get involved and fight for the changes that are needed to turn from a reactionary, unbalanced democracy to a democracy that is progressive, visionary, and balanced. For some, involvement will be a commitment to serve and effect the changes demanded by the people. These individuals will surface to run for government offices. For the rest, getting involved will be as simple as registering and voting for those with integrity and statesmanship who will commit to change.

2.4   Voting Machines

Another of the most sacred acts in a democracy is the responsibility to ensure that the votes cast in any election are properly counted and the actual votes cast are those that are counted. The use of voting processes or machines that leave a paper trail effectively accomplish this assurance. However, in modern elections, voting machines have been utilized in several instances that do not leave a paper trail, and, worse yet, the machines have been proven to allow their vote counts to be manipulated electronically. In a democracy the use of such machines must be outlawed from use in any election. The use of these machines has allowed some people to virtually guarantee an election to a candidate, with the candidate generally being from the minority party.

Any voting machines or electronic equipment used for voters to cast their votes must be beyond reproach as to accuracy and tampering. When electronic voting machines have no backup system to verify the original votes cast, the democratic system has failed. When electronic voting machines use cards to collect the votes and data, and the cards can be altered to produce a different result than what was cast by the voters, the democratic system has failed. When electronic voting equipment is put in place without concrete assurances that the equipment is backed up and tamperproof, the temptation for a minority party to alter the results is far too great and therefore must be totally eliminated. This practice of cheating with voting machines is akin to stealing an election and, with a government of the majority under a Social Capitalist economic system, must be constitutionally banned.

2.5   Electoral College

The Electoral College for selection of the president of the United States no longer serves a purpose that can't be better served by direct election. One of the original intents of the Electoral College was to ensure that the president would be officially selected by the elite, as in unfettered capitalists, not the excitable masses, who were seen as illiterate and uneducated. The Electoral College system was also a means by which word of the popular vote in the country could be relayed to the capital in an orderly fashion. Times have changed, and the masses are no longer excitable, illiterate, and uneducated. Mass communication now relays the election results quickly to the entire nation. The purpose of the Electoral College is clearly out of step with the times and with a true democracy.

If it is intended that the intellectual elite would have the final say in selection of the president, these same people would defend retention of the Electoral College. If it is intended that the people should choose the president by popular vote, and the Electoral College was only a means to relay the message, then there is no question as to elimination of the Electoral College in favor of a popular vote. In either event, it is time to recognize that every voice in a democracy must be heard. This can only be accomplished by direct election of the president through the popular vote. With a government of the majority under a Social Capitalist economic system, the Electoral College must be eliminated through a constitutional amendment in favor of directly electing a president.

The Electoral College as established by the Constitution is no longer necessary to facilitate democracy. The electoral system, as previously stated, was set in place by the elite (capitalists) under the premise of having to get the popular vote outcome from the states to the capital during a time of horse and buggy transportation. With the Electoral College, the elite would naturally control the selection of the electors. They further ensured control by providing that electors are pledged and not constitutionally bound to support the candidate selected by the popular vote in their state. By being simply pledged, the electors have no criminal or constitutional penalty for breaking a pledge.

Without question, the deck is stacked in favor of the elite having the final say in the selection of the president.

With the mass transit and telecommunications of today, coupled with the majority of the masses being literate and educated, the premises for establishing the Electoral College are obsolete. It is time to abolish the Electoral College through a constitutional amendment and revert to the popular vote for selection of a president. This move will create a truly democratic system for electing the president, not a disguised charade perpetrated on the people as being democratic. It would eventually reestablish faith in the voting system and increase voter turnout. It would give every individual vote a meaning, instead of being viewed as a frivolous act.

As a popular vote is established for selection of the president, the news media must be restrained from reporting election results prematurely. To provide equality in voter perception and participation, reporting results for presidential or congressional candidates must not be released until all the polls have closed. Every individual must be treated equally in the casting of their ballot, which is mutually excluded when standings are available prior to the closing of all the polls. If this method requires staggering the voting times to facilitate the uniform closing of polls, then it must be implemented. The fair exercising of the right and privilege to vote must take precedence over the wishes of the media.

2.6   Career Politicians/Term Limits

Where in the US Constitution is it written that the nation will be led by career politicians? In fact, a case can be made for the very opposite. The US Constitution provides for the election of representatives to Congress and for the election of the president. However, it provided for the appointment for life of members to the Supreme Court. The founding fathers intended that the shadows in the halls of Congress would be constantly changing, in recognition of a dynamic institution. If the founding fathers had intended for Congress to have career politicians, why then only two- and six-year terms? Why not ten-, twelve-, or twenty-year terms? Truly, the intent was for turnover, without favor given to an incumbent to live and retire as a member of Congress and draw unconscionable perks and a retirement off the taxpayers. Career politicians, especially those that have chosen politics as a career right out of school, can be detached from the reality of the working class, having never had to work for a living. It seems that the intent of the US Constitution was to select candidates for Congress that had real jobs and elect them to Congress to enact laws based on experience.

Politicians who have been making politics a career can lose touch with the needs of the working class and become unduly influenced by corporate special interest lobbyists.

The nation chose to limit anyone elected president to no more than two four-year terms by passage of the Twenty-Second Amendment to the US Constitution. Why should a similar limit not be applied to the members of Congress? Term limits for the members of Congress should be enacted in the interest of greater participation and integrity in government. A member of Congress should serve this nation by upholding the purpose of the federal government, to protect the public interest, not by promoting powerful special interests.

"No man is good enough to govern another man without that other's consent."
—Abraham Lincoln

There should be an outcry by the people for limited terms for the members of Congress so that government will be run in a businesslike manner and in the interest of the people. Members are needed in Congress who will serve and stand on their records, instead of making partisan political decisions that will ensure reelection. More importantly, limited terms are necessary in order to lessen the stranglehold of influential members of Congress who believe they are the only ones who know what is best for the people, and who are determined to perpetuate their reelections. The US Constitution intended that the states would be equally represented in the Senate and proportionately represented in the House of Representatives. The US Constitution also provided that each house of Congress would set its own rules. The rules established for the selection of chairmen/women of the numerous congressional committees is generally by seniority within the majority party controlling the chamber. This favors senior incumbents at the expense of newly elected members. In addition, the power over a committee vested in the chair can determine if a bill presented by anyone on the committee will be acted upon. This power can also invoke inequality among the members of Congress. It is the abuse or potential abuse of this power and influence that justifies a cry for limiting the terms of congressional members in order to bring an air of balance or equality to Congress. The selection of congressional committee chairpersons should be changed so that the power to allow bills to move through committees is not vested in a single or a few individuals.

Through incumbency and reelection posturing, most politicians serve themselves and their reelection more than the interests of the people.

Another primary reason to limit the terms of the members of Congress is to minimize or eliminate the posturing for reelection that engulfs the legislative process. The term for a representative should be doubled to four years. All members of Congress should then be held to no more than one term of service. Senators and representatives would thereby no longer have to posture for reelection. If there is to be a statesmanlike government, members elected to Congress could actually spend their time on legislative matters as opposed to constant fund raising for reelection.

Politicians spend an enormous amount of time and money simply posturing for reelection. They become so entwined in the system that they are susceptible to the whims of those with money and influence to gain help from them in financing their future campaigns. This is not democracy. It is capitalist democracy, where those who own the means of production and distribution would also try to own the means of regulation over such production and distribution. What chance does the working class have in such a system? Are the working class equally represented? Incumbency and the need for money can perpetuate the will of influence and power, not the will of the people. When politicians are more concerned with making the choices that will provide dollars for reelection, rather than the needs of the people, the entire system has failed.

Limiting terms for the members of the United States Congress has been discussed for quite some time. The proposal for limited terms is entirely logical. The elected politician—who, having been elected by the people, will serve as the representative of those people and then pursue reelection in his or her own interest—cannot be blamed. However, politicians can be blamed for putting their own interests ahead of the interests of the people, under the pretense of serving the people. Though one is elected, it is a lack of integrity and statesmanship that casts a vote against the majority, however rationalized. This is the type of politics that has justified the call for limited terms. A democracy doesn't need career politicians; it needs statesmen and stateswomen serving in government.

To the same end, the more that a problem is discussed among various individuals with differing viewpoints, the greater the potential for reaching the correct legislative solution. As is true for most products, the more the purpose of the product or idea is filtered, the finer or more pure the final product becomes. It is the same for solutions to problems. In government, differing views on any given subject that may need legislative action may be talked about for years before anything is done. The same views are continually discussed among the same members of Congress, without change or input from other sources. If there were limited terms for the members of Congress, and turnover in congressional staff, there would be a greater possibility of legislative solutions being closer to the best possible solution.

A paramount obstacle to the enactment of good legislation is the flow of "chips" in government. Chips in Washington, as in poker, are collected and then cashed in when the holder so chooses. In poker, you win chips by having the best hand in the particular game, and you cash them in for money of equal value. It is quite the same in Washington. If a given member of Congress, or even the president, has a bill that is highly desired but not supported by the interests of the majority, he or she will offer "chips" in return for support of the bill.

> *Politicians may have to use "chips" (favors) in the legislative process to get their bills passed.*

What are these chips? Chips are promises to act. They are favors that, once given out, can be called back when support is needed. For instance, if the president wants to pass a particular bill and has strong support but not enough to pass the bill, he will approach a number of the members of Congress who may be undecided or open to being persuaded. He may request their support on this bill in return for a future act in favor of the member. If the member agrees to act in favor of the president, he or she is said to now have a chip from the president. In other words, the president now "owes" him or her one. Such a chip may be "called in" by the holder in the future in order to get appropriate action on a bill that he or she favors or dislikes.

Chips are more frequent in Congress between the members. "You support my bill and I'll support your bill" is the game. If both bills are not on the floor at the same time, one or the other of the members has a chip until the second bill surfaces, at which time the chip is called. Are chips used on all legislation? No! Does every member of Congress use chips? Not necessarily! Are all chips bad for the public interest? Not necessarily! The point is that if the members of Congress and the president were statesmen or stateswomen, they wouldn't need chips. Legislation would be logical and in the interest of the majority, not special interests that need favors to get it enacted. Unfortunately, when partisan politics is the norm, and when negotiation, compromise, and communication are absent, bribery, as in chips, is a solution.

Statesmen and stateswomen in government would not allow themselves to be reduced to the use of chips. If the only way to gain support for legislation is through chips, the legislation is usually flawed from the beginning and should not be imposed upon the people. Government officials must recognize that logical reasoning and not chips must be provided in service to the people. Chips and favors in government must be replaced by integrity, statesmanship/stateswomanship, and logical reasoning. Anything short of this change is an effort in futility and will only perpetuate the existing flawed system. The voters must see that those who serve have the qualities that eliminate the potential of resorting to the use of chips in serving the public. Chips, generally, will guarantee that the taxpayer is once again stuck with the bill for bad legislation. Getting capitalist money out of the election process and adoption of Social Capitalism can go a long way toward getting chips out of the legislative process.

2.7   Publicly Financed Campaigns

Political campaigns are expensive. Even with integrity, candidates must still get their message across to the voters. It takes money to get the message out. Once money puts candidates in office, it can also keep them there. As wealth and political influence are accumulated by incumbents, they have an advantage over any nonincumbent. There is no longer equal access to the position that is up for election. Private money taints the political process. Running for a national office in a democracy is so expensive that only the wealthy capitalists or those with capitalist backers can generally afford to run. Therefore, all campaigns for the presidency or Congress should be at public expense. With as little as $5 to $10 of public funding per taxpayer, all federal elections would provide equal access and equal opportunity, whether incumbent or not. The working class deserves equal treatment, opportunity, and access to the political process. Public financing of campaigns can provide equal opportunity to participate in politics. Public financing of campaigns in place of privately purchased politicians minimizes special interest influence, for the betterment of a majority of the people. Public financing could also encourage statesmen/women to serve the nation rather than just the wealthy.

The news media must be required to provide equal access to the candidates at little or no cost. Limiting terms is one stopgap measure to address the unequal access to the media in pursuit of election. Incumbents tend to get caught up in the power that is government and lose sight of the fact that they are not the only ones who can serve the nation. The system was intended to provide the opportunity for new thoughts and innovation. Statesmanship and stateswomanship with equal access, or limited terms, will provide that which was intended.

The chance to serve the people as president or as a member of Congress must be available to any qualified person who offers to serve. A Social Capitalist economic system could provide that opportunity. Such a system would provide for those who would serve as statesmen and stateswomen, vowing to serve the needs of the majority. Regardless of the chamber from which a legislative bill emerged, or who got credit for sponsoring it, these people would vow to do that which is right for the majority working class. Their voting records would stand on their own, and the voters would react accordingly in future elections. All Congressional voting records must be published locally and easily accessible on the internet. It would require that people who are fed up with politics as usual get involved in selecting those who will serve the people in government.

Elected officials must ensure that the interests of those represented, and not the special interests of those with the means to influence staff, are upheld. The general public does not have the financial means to affect legislation to the degree that special interest lobbyists with influence and money can. It is the interest of the public that will suffer when money and lobbyists are involved in the legislative process. Elected officials must ensure that equal opportunity is afforded the public by both themselves and their staff. The development of publicly financed campaigns under a Social Capitalist economic system would reduce the degree to which special interests could affect the lives of the public without the public's knowledge. Without a declared equal economic opportunity policy, it is easier for congressional staff to be steered or be swayed by special interest lobbyists toward other than the public interest. Without a declared Social Capitalist economic system, neither the public nor members of Congress have any means by which to measure the claims by special interests of how they interpret the economic impact of any given legislation. Together with posturing for reelection, this makes it easier for some members of Congress or their staffs to ignore the public interest. Without publicly financed campaigns, the public is less able to recognize what their representation is doing and hold them accountable. A Social Capitalist economic system would provide for the elimination of lobbyists from the political arena as another control over greed.

"In a republican nation, whose citizens are to be led by reason and persuasion and not by force, the art of reasoning becomes of first importance."
                                              —Thomas Jefferson

3. Taxation

A democracy will only survive through the full employment of the working class at a living wage in the private or public sector. Any policy that deviates from this premise is nonprogressive and will eventually result in taxation of the working class beyond their capacity to endure. It is the capitalists and working class that provide tax dollars to the government. The working class receives the paychecks that pay the taxes and purchase the products from which businesses produce, pay taxes, and enjoy a profit. It is the capitalists that pay taxes on their profits. These taxes provide the tax dollars that the government spends on defense, programs for the less fortunate, procurements, and other programs. When capitalists continue to cut taxes on the wealthy, the capitalists are sending a message that they do not want to support the civilized nation in providing for the less fortunate, for health care for everyone, for defense of the nation, for the care of veterans, for the upgrading of infrastructure and roads, etc. They are only interested in the accumulation of obscene wealth under an unfettered capitalist economic system that allows them to get away with such hoarding of wealth.

When an income tax system is imposed on a nation's people, a very important aspect of the system must be acknowledged and implemented also. That aspect is the opportunity of employment being guaranteed to all of the working class, regardless of their location or stature in life. How can there be a mandated income tax when there is no guarantee of employment? How can those who earn a living be asked to support those that do not? How can those who would extract millions of dollars in salaries, bonuses, or profits from an unfettered capitalist economic system have no social responsibility or pay little or nothing in taxes? The government must introduce a full employment policy. This employment policy must recognize that private and public sector jobs are the backbone of an economy. Capitalists try to impress upon the nation that their money is the backbone of the economy. This impression is false. Capitalist money is utilized by capitalists to make more money any way they can. It is the working class, which includes small businesses, that is the backbone of a nation's economy. When the working class is employed at a living wage and benefits, the money they earn is spent on improving their lifestyle. It is this spending that fuels the economy. Capitalists hoard their money that is attained through unfettered capitalism policy. This money is shielded from taxation and thereby removed from the economy, which creates unemployment and a suppressed economy. The government, in the interest of the public, must provide through its tax policy the incentives that will encourage private sector employment for everyone in the working class under a Social Capitalist economic system.

With an unfettered capitalist economy, most capitalists become wealthy at the expense of or by the efforts of the noncapitalist working class. To give nothing back to those less fortunate is undemocratic, not in keeping with the essence of life, and unpatriotic. This situation is perpetuated by the lack of a declared Social Capitalist economic policy and equal economic opportunity. Granted, there are many capitalists who have done wonders in making life better for the less fortunate, but there are many more that have not. If the capitalists will not voluntarily support the economy that allowed them to become capitalists, then government must provide incentives or taxation to do it for them. The capitalist elite must be induced to contribute support, or to put every able-bodied American to work. At the same time the capitalists should not complain when the government enacts laws that would take back, through taxation, some of the wealth that the unfettered capitalism system allowed them to accumulate. The capitalists do not need governmental protections to the same degree as the working class. The capitalists have the means to protect their interests; the working class does not. The incentive to better oneself through the accumulation of wealth by legitimate means must not be infringed or unjustly obstructed but equally, must not be unfettered.

Why then is it not the policy of government to have full employment of the working class? A full employment policy and the incentives to the private sector to expand, develop, and create new jobs are essential. Anything short of a full employment policy and the necessary incentives to achieve it is self-serving of those who enjoy an exorbitant lifestyle at the expense of the working class. A movement like the pledge of "no new taxes," signed onto by many politicians, is another selfish practice of the capitalists.

Capitalists must also be required to pay their share of taxes in return for the privilege of capital accumulation. When a progressive income tax is established along with an inheritance tax, they both are designed just as they should be in a democracy. It has been the capitalists over time that have continued to push for reduced taxation on the wealthy and elimination of the inheritance tax. In a capitalist democracy, the taxation should be in relation to the income. In addition, the inheritance or estate tax is a proper check and balance on the greed of unfettered capitalism to temper the "rich getting richer" and the "poor getting poorer." Elimination of the estate tax is just another ploy by capitalists to accumulate wealth way beyond reason or need. The solution is a Social Capitalist economic system with full employment through the taxation of the private sector, with tax credits or rebates based on employment levels afforded the capitalists, corporations, and businesses.

Living in a democracy leads people to believe that they have hope for a better life. Hope is available if there is opportunity, and specifically the opportunity for employment. It is the responsibility of government to ensure the opportunity for employment, thus giving everyone hope. Without opportunity there is hopelessness, crime, lack of self-esteem, racism, etc. The government can use the taxation system to ensure full employment for everyone.

There must be logical incentives that will enhance employment and job creation, and stop the ridiculous government spending policies utilized to bolster the economy as is currently exercised. Ridiculous government spending policies include "too big to fail bank" bailouts, first time homebuyer subsidizes, and buying and destroying old cars. Once employment is maximized, everything else falls in order, including a maximized tax base to pay for government programs. Even then, the cost of the incentives does not increase the expenditure of tax dollars. Rather, they decrease tax dollar expenditures in the long term by shifting the support from taxpayers, through unemployment and welfare, to the private sector through full employment at a living wage and benefits.

The income tax in a democracy is the tool with which the government sees to it that services are provided to the people. Tax policy must be utilized to ensure that the private sector, as much as possible, provides the services for the people. Tax policy must be utilized to ensure that those who benefit most from capitalism also have a social responsibility to ensure provision for all. This social responsibility must be a combination of employment at a living wage and through taxation to provide for the unemployed with a Social Capitalist economic system. Capitalists, corporations, and businesses must be taxed at rates substantially higher than the working class, afforded business expense deductions, provided with tax incentives to induce employment, and provided tax credits or rebates based on employment levels at a living wage and benefits. Minimum wages must be expanded to provide that adults will earn a living wage and benefits. Attention must be given to the measures that will create jobs, such as enterprise zones, capital gains tax rates for employment only, investment credits, employment credits, public infrastructure construction, and others that will ensure employment and jobs for all.

An important key to the success of the American economy is obtaining the maximum tax base possible. There will not be a maximum tax base unless all of the working class is employed at a living wage and benefits. Capitalists and corporations must also be held responsible for paying their fair share of taxes so that the tax burden is not shouldered solely by the working class. There is no place in America for the North American Free Trade Agreement (NAFTA) and Central American Free Trade Agreement (CAFTA) or any other free trade agreements when the sole purpose is to provide cheap labor to the capitalists at the expense of working class jobs. In fact, free trade agreements should be illegal and fair trade agreements should be the standard. The jobs shipped out of a country through offshoring or offshore outsourcing in order to enhance the profits of capitalists are exactly why a democratic nation needs a Social Capitalist economic system.

> *"In order that the extra rich can become so affluent, they must necessarily take more of what ordinarily would belong to the average man."*
> —Plato

The most significant changes in the American tax structure began with Reaganomics. Reaganomics stressed tax cuts for the wealthy and a trickle-down economy, which began the stockpiling of ill-gotten profits by capitalists. In other words, if capitalists are rich, the working class may survive. The acts formulated under his watch included the Economic Recovery Act of 1981, also known as the Kemp-Roth Tax Act, which cut taxes mainly on the wealthy in America to the tune of $1.441 trillion over eight years. Without this act, in 1989 the taxpayers would have had a budget surplus of an estimated $120 billion instead of trillions in debt. The acts also included the Tax Reform Act of 1986, which removed any incentives for businesses to employ or create jobs, and spending on defense so flagrant that the Pentagon couldn't spend all the money without atrocious stockpiles of unneeded materials. Reagan's legacy lives on in recent administrations, which have chosen to perpetuate the practice of tax cuts for the wealthy under the pretense that it will bolster the economy. The only things that are bolstered by tax cuts for the wealthy are the stock market and the offshore bank accounts of the capitalists.

A Social Capitalist economic system must include that an ill-gotten gains or wealth tax be imposed on all income obtained by capitalists as a result of Reaganomics, subsequent tax cuts, and deregulation. Senator Huey P. Long of Louisiana, in his plan to "Share Our Wealth," proposed a cap on personal fortunes or wealth. Such a cap must be put in place under Social Capitalism. Such an action could nearly eliminate the national debt. In concert with this action there should be set in place a national tax credit for all employment at a federally determined living wage and benefits. This employment tax credit would enhance the profits for corporations and businesses since their taxes would have been significantly increased under Social Capitalism. In addition, the deregulation of stock market speculation that results in manipulation of commodities and futures trading must be rescinded. When banks and speculators can manipulate prices that result in massive profits to the banks and speculators at tremendous costs to the public, the system screams for regulation.

*"In the councils of government, we must guard against
the acquisition of unwarranted influence, whether
sought or unsought, by the military industrial complex."*
—Dwight D. Eisenhower

4.   National Defense

Everyone, regardless of his or her class in life, supports the men
and women serving in the armed forces of the United States.
However, this will not stop politicians from posturing for reelection
by implying that they and their party support the men and
women in the armed forces more than anyone else. Not everyone
in a democracy supports the capitalists who take a nation into a
remote war to secure oil profits for the capitalists. Under unfettered
capitalism, the capitalists view war as good business from which to
profit. It is a sad day for democracy when military men and women
are sent to their death in a foreign land when there is no evidence
that there was a threat to the nation. In many cases, due to the lack
of a Social Capitalist economic system that would provide a decent
standard of living for the working class, young men and women join
the military for the benefits of higher education in the hopes that
they can better themselves. Wealthy families do not have to have
their children join the service in hopes of getting a higher education.
In reality, this is unfair to the working class and especially minorities.
Furthermore, it is shameful that the military heroes that fall or are
wounded in that war are not honored when they are brought home,
as they have been in previous justified wars. It is even more shameful
and unpatriotic that capitalists want to eliminate the taxes on the
wealthy that would be used to provide medical care and assistance to
the veterans of such oil wars.

***There must be election of a president who will control
the military and military spending to what is necessary***

under a Social Capitalist economic system, not what the military have become accustomed to through waste, fraud, and abuse.

A military requires an immense annual budget. The products, material, and ordnance that are developed from the funding are absolutely justified when they go to that which protects military personnel and provides the extraordinary advanced technology equipment to gain an advantage in military undertakings. The funding is not justified when it goes for waste, fraud, or abuse. With a Social Capitalist economic system, it would be possible to create a clearinghouse for all defense spending that would ensure that procurements are properly conducted, competitive, and only contracted if the product or service is not already available. In addition, it would ensure wherever possible that defense contracts are open and competitive and not sole sourced. Finally, a Social Capitalist economic system would ensure that any future wars are absolutely necessary and properly authorized to protect the nation.

4.1   Veterans

> *"The tree of liberty grows only when watered by the blood of tyrants."*
> —Bertrand Barere

Veterans must be treated with the utmost respect since democratic freedom is enjoyed at the expense of those who fought to preserve freedom. They should not have to be in need of any of life's necessities for the rest of their lives. It is appalling to see a government continue to require veterans to beg for the necessities of life, including medical care in less than desirable veterans' hospitals. If a nation can afford to spend billions on preparing for war, and on tax cuts for the rich, it can afford to spend whatever it takes to make sure that veterans are cared for during the rest of their lives. Capitalists and those that capitalize and profiteer on war through manufacturing and selling to the military must share substantially in the welfare of veterans through taxation.

Not all veterans need help with all the necessities of life. Some need more than others, while some will need no help at all except the recognition and thanks of the people they fought to defend. If veterans are going to be required to use veterans' hospitals, these hospitals should be the epitome of the medical profession. If it requires the closing or sale of a military golf course in order to upgrade veterans' hospitals and provide whatever services are necessary, then it must be done.

No country should send its citizens into combat without ample provision taken for their return and the care that will be required in all aspects of their future. There must continue to be a provision to give veterans preference in hiring and also to fund veterans' benefit programs, such as housing and educational opportunities. There are holidays to honor and commemorate those who have fought or fallen in the defense of freedom and indeed the rest of the world. All such programs and commemorations must be revisited regularly under a Social Capitalist economic system to ensure that the needs of all veterans are being met adequately.

Veterans have not been afforded the gratitude, respect, and services deserved by those who fought for freedom and democracy, while others enjoyed life or profiteered from defense spending.

A Social Capitalist economic system would include a full employment policy and provide for the full employment and care of veterans. Changes in policies that would contribute to the eradication of racism, discrimination, and homelessness, among others, will also help to promote the respect due all veterans. A national health care system would provide medical treatment for any veteran at any facility in the nation. In short, every veteran has more than earned the respect of everyone who resides in a free society as a result of their sacrifice. Simple gratitude is insufficient. Gratitude must permeate every aspect of contact between the public and veterans. Respect is earned, not commanded, and veterans have earned the respect of everyone in the nation, including the government. Social Capitalism will ensure that the funding for veteran programs is considered before extravagant officers' clubs and military golf courses. It will also ensure through tax policy that the wealthy, who benefit proportionately more than the rest from war, pay their fair share to support the military and veterans programs.

"The whole of government consists in the art of being honest."

—Thomas Jefferson

5. National Debt

In America, there is considerable concern over the annual federal budget deficit and the size of the national debt. However, these are not the only concerns, nor the greatest concerns facing America, contrary to what the capitalists would lead the people to believe. By concentrating all the attention on the supposed immediate need to balance the budget and begin reducing the national debt, attention is drawn away from the primary concern, which should be expansion of private sector employment and the creation of jobs. What does an unemployed head of a household care about a deficit or debt, if there is no job or income with which to feed a family? It is not surprising that during capitalist government administrations, there is little mention of the national debt and deficit while the nation is spent into tremendous additional debt. However, when a majority administration is elected, it is the capitalists that determine now is the time to cut the deficit and national debt by cutting Social Security, Medicare, Medicaid, and other social programs but have no problem with additional tax cuts for the wealthy. This is a significant reason that a democratic nation must have a Social Capitalist economic system for the protection of all. Greedy capitalists stress the need to reduce the deficit and debt only to make room for more tax cuts for the wealthy. In fact, if the capitalists stressed full employment and worked to make it happen, the economy would boom, their profits would go up, and the deficit and debt would go down. Unfortunately the greedy capitalists are only interested in their obscene wealth at the expense of the working class.

The time for a balanced budget is not when expansion is needed in order to improve the economy. Once a stable economy is achieved, it may be possible to live with a balanced budget. The time for a balanced budget is when the economy has stabilized with full employment. In the meantime, efforts to achieve a balanced budget or reduce the national debt must be in the area of eliminating waste, fraud, and abuse in government spending, and maximizing the tax base, all of which is entirely possible. In addition, corporate welfare, such as the billions of dollars in oil subsidies, must be eliminated.

Complete elimination of the deficit and the national debt, with the existing policies of the government still in place, would not ensure there would be full employment. There are still no incentives for businesses to expand or to create jobs. It cannot be assumed that, because the debt is eliminated, there will therefore be more money to be put into business expansion and job creation. This assumption has already been proven false by the failed trickle-down economic theory. Tax breaks were given to businesses, but without incentives to invest in job creation, the necessary expansion did not result. The capitalists would like to have the people think that elimination of the national debt would free up trillions of dollars so the economy will prosper. In reality, without the proper incentives in place, it will not happen. The stock market will soar and secure interest-bearing investments will soar, but without incentives the situation of the working class, less fortunate, and unemployed will not change, and therefore some social programs need to continue. The proper first step in elimination of the annual deficit and national debt is job creation incentives of every possible nature to the private sector, coupled with tax increases on the wealthy. To enhance full employment, the government can invest in public infrastructure projects such as rebuilding bridges, roads, schools, public transportation, and water/sewer systems.

An area that has been under discussion as a constitutional amendment is to provide for a balanced federal budget. It is convenient for capitalists to focus public attention on the supposed dire need for a balanced budget as a diversion from having to address the real issues. It is the economic system that has failed. There are numerous other measures that can and must be set in motion that will decrease the national debt and diminish the need for any balanced budget amendment. To have created trillions of dollars in annual deficits and national debt through obscene tax cuts for the wealthy and defense spending, and then to call for a balanced budget to repair the damage, cannot be justified. The defense buildup, unnecessary wars, and illogical economic policies must not be shouldered by the working class, who are already burdened by the original incompetent acts.

An unbalanced budget is the product of failed economic policy. When the government has to provide for the working class, underserved, unemployed, and indigent because capitalists are not required to provide for them under an unfettered capitalism economic system, the result is an unbalanced budget. Capitalists would have the people believe that to reduce the national debt, there should be greater tax cuts for the wealthy along with higher taxes on the working class. In addition, these same capitalists would reduce federal spending by elimination of social programs like Social Security and Medicare. The proper change to reduce the national debt is to make the change from the greed-ridden unfettered capitalist economic system to Social Capitalism, which would include increasing taxes on the wealthy, full employment of the working class at living wages and benefits, and increased regulation of capitalist greed.

During a period when the economy is in chaos, it isn't proper to begin a revision of policy that would curtail jobs in favor of reducing the annual deficit or national debt.

The emphasis must be on the reform of economic policy to create jobs, not on trickle-down Reaganomics that benefits the elite and burdens multitudes for decades to come. Employment and job creation incentives that will bring the economy to prosperity for all must be implemented immediately. Full employment incentives, government-guaranteed loans, enterprise zones, tax policy that enhances employment, and a buy-American program are all incentives that can be enacted to address the deficit and national debt. Capitalists have no interest in providing the leadership that would set these policies in motion. The working class majority party is the only hope for the responsible leadership that will provide the change to a Social Capitalist economic system and the policy changes needed in a democracy.

> *Social programs in a democracy of equals are necessitated by the failure of an economic system that does not provide equal economic opportunity for all.*

It is not spending on social programs that is wrong; it is the lack of a full employment policy that necessitated social spending. Although capitalists have gained politically by blaming spending on social programs, capitalists as the recognized representatives of the wealthy are actually more at fault. Capitalists have failed to provide for the working class as is endorsed under capitalism. Elite capitalists want to have their cake and eat it, too. With unfettered capitalism, neither the businesses nor the government provides full employment of the working class, which would be socially responsible and would minimize the need for government spending on social programs. Then, when the government provides for the unemployed through social programs funded by taxation, capitalists don't want to be taxed to fund the programs either. The working class have had to do that which is absolutely correct by supporting social programs that provide for the working class, which capitalists and businesses have refused to provide.

Massive social spending is necessitated for lack of a full employment policy. A Social Capitalist economic system would have significantly reduced the need for social spending. The failure to have delegated a social responsibility to the capitalists and employers under the economic system is why a Social Capitalist economic system must be adopted for a democracy. The national debt is the failure to recognize there are three economic partners—capitalists, the working class, and government—all of whom must be treated as equals in order to keep capitalist greed from hoarding the money that should be paying the living wages and benefits that would have further reduced the need for social programs.

"The preservation of health is a duty. Few seem conscious that there is such a thing as physical morality."
—Herbert Spencer

6. Health Care

Defense spending, police protection, fire protection, and education, among other programs, are basically social programs provided by a democratic government. National health care must be added to the government programs available to all in a democracy. The primary reason that health care hasn't evolved into a government program is that the capitalists make huge profits from providing health care. Insurance companies, medical facilities, drug companies, and others all rake in obscene profits from the misery of others. This practice is immoral and unjust. National health care under a Social Capitalist economic system can be a reality without a major overhaul of the existing system.

The answer is found in the need to move to an equal opportunity economic system under Social Capitalism, and in the evolution of other public policies in a democracy. Look at education, police protection, fire protection, and utilities. For lack of a Social Capitalist system, in most of these cases it was determined to be in the public interest to provide these services. Public education and protections were provided at public expense in the best interest of the people. Utilities, on the other hand, were supplied through sole source suppliers with government assistance and assurances. It is pretty obvious by now the decisions were in the best interest of the public for these services to have been provided in such a manner. Nearly every family in a democracy has police protection, fire protection of some sort, electrical service, and guaranteed public education opportunities. All of these services were determined to be in the best interest of having a healthy population, and it was determined that they should be made available at public expense. Why, then, if these essential social services were necessary for the health of the public and thereby publicly provided, wasn't the most direct provision for the health of the public not provided in a similar manner? In his writings on capitalism, Adam Smith wrote that government has the duty of "erecting and maintaining those public institutions and those public works which may be in the highest degree advantageous to a great society." National health care fits as a public institution of the highest order.

6.1   National Health Care

National health care has become a significant issue, and rightfully so. Each year, billions of dollars are spent on the preservation of freedom for citizens to pursue life, liberty, and happiness. Career politicians provide for their own health care and well-being in a manner that can only be envied. Most certainly, then, a democracy can provide for all the people to be free of undue suffering for want of complete health care coverage.

> *Universal national health care, as in Medicare and Medicaid, must be made available to all as a public service and is as logical as public education and police protection, especially within an unequal economic system that does not provide equal economic opportunity for all; it is only the evolution of the system and greedy capitalists that have kept it from being so.*

It is time in a democratic nation for complete health care coverage to be made available to every citizen. To support the cost of such a provision, several factions of the economy that are now providing insurance protection policies would contribute support to the public cost. For instance, there is currently a significant duplication or near duplication of health insurances carried by many individuals and families. This duplication is found when an individual has private health insurance, health insurance provided as an employee benefit, workers' compensation insurance, Medicare, Medicaid, automobile medical insurance coverage, and any number of other specific insurance coverages. Usually the premiums are paid to an insurance company that takes a profit and sees that the services are provided when needed. If the system reverted to a universal national health care government system, then complete health care coverage would be provided for everyone. Social Capitalism would require that all employers provide, in addition to a living wage, family health care coverage by paying into the universal national health care government system. When national health care coverage is provided, the employers would pay into the government program based on the number of employees.

Under a national health care government system, Medicare and Medicaid funding as now appropriated would be contributed to the system for all. Employers and businesses would pay a single specified amount per employee to the system, in recognition of no longer having to seek insurance coverage as a benefit to employees. In addition, the medical portion of workers' compensation insurance could be eliminated. Equally, with a full employment economic policy also in place, workers' compensation could be revised to remove medical coverage with the unemployment provision of the full employment policy providing for any lost time by an employee. Every other insurance policy, such as homeowners' and automobile insurance, executed in the nation would provide a specific contribution to the national health care system, recognizing that there is no longer a need for medical coverage in the policy. Private insurance coverage could still be available for those who could afford it, but it would only be needed to cover that which isn't provided for by the national Medicare/Medicaid health care system.

National health care must provide every citizen with equal access, with the medical profession encouraged to provide services at a reasonable cost. The spirit of innovation and invention in the fields of medicine must not be impeded. Rather, an incentive for providing services must be pursued, if necessary, through governmental oversight. Entry into the medical profession, by the very nature of the demand on one's abilities and time, should provide a reasonable reward. However, the pursuit of a medical profession under Social Capitalism should first be service rather than reward.

A democracy needs doctors and hospitals, and governmental assurances if necessary, to ensure that no individual will be denied medical attention. It is stated in the US Constitution that every citizen shall have the right to life, liberty, and the pursuit of happiness. It does not state that only those who can afford it have the right to life, liberty, and the pursuit of happiness. Ample evidence exists from which to develop a premise that justifies national health care as good public policy. In many nations on this earth, the right to health care is already assured. Why should a great democratic nation, a leader in technology, a vanguard of freedom, provide less for its citizens? What is the meaning of freedom if the people shall fall for lack of adequate health care?

The capitalist economic system in a democracy provides that the elite capitalists can afford health coverage by virtue of their control over the wealth of the nation. Government employees and elected officials are provided with reasonable health care protection by virtue of their access to the taxpayers' pocketbook. Who, then, provides health care coverage for the working class, the unemployed, and the homeless? The working class, as already stated, is the fuel that makes the economy and government able to operate and makes the capitalists wealthy. For those of the working class who are lucky enough to have jobs that provide healthcare coverage as a benefit, the problem is less severe, until they lose their jobs or the benefit is eliminated. For the unemployed and unemployable, there is no such coverage except at government expense anyway. It is time to make the system fair for all, and take the fear of an existence without health care coverage out of the formula for the pursuit of happiness. Such a provision is as important for the future of all in a democracy as the provision of a policy of full employment. With a universal national Medicare/Medicaid health care system, the integrity of the program must be closely monitored to eliminate waste, fraud, abuse, and profiteering. Random independent audits of the charges would be a means of assurance.

6.2   Medicare/Medicaid

Medicare/Medicaid under a universal program must become the national health care program for all Americans. Even with a national full employment policy at a living wage and benefits, when the working class employees retire, they will still need health care. Therefore, the Medicare/Medicaid program must not only be continued but expanded to cover all Americans. If Congress can provide health care for life to themselves, their families, the presidents and vice presidents, then equal treatment must be afforded the rest of the population under a Social Capitalist economic system. Medicare/Medicaid must never be converted to a voucher program under any circumstances. A Medicare/Medicaid voucher program is just another avenue for the greedy capitalists to get their hands in the taxpayers' cookie jar to accumulate more obscene wealth.

6.3   Regionalization

A universal government system of covering health care costs can prove much more efficient and cost effective than when paid through insurance companies. With private insurances paying the bills, nearly every medical facility is set up to handle nearly any medical procedure that would possibly be encountered. This is a result of each facility being a complete independent provider. Under a universal system, to ensure the best value for dollars spent, regional systems should be set up. Within each region, different facilities could specialize in different medical procedures. This would provide for greater utilization of very expensive medical equipment, which would reduce the cost of medical care for all. Such regionalization could result in a single piece of equipment being purchased and used nearly 100 percent of the time rather than having several pieces in the region, each of which is used only part time. Regionalization could provide for the temporary assignment of doctors and nurses to other than their own facilities in the event of a natural disaster or significant emergency. In any event, regionalization would ensure the availability of complete medical coverage to all, regardless of where they live.

Regionalization would provide for full services to remote areas which may otherwise have problems supporting complete medical facilities.

With regionalization as the standard, every area of the nation would be in a region. The problems experienced in recent years with a lack of interest in providing medical services in rural areas would be eliminated. Each region would determine the method of ensuring that services are provided to every individual in the region, whether urban or rural. Limited service facilities in rural areas could be supplemented with full service facilities in the population centers. Medical evacuation helicopters could be used for emergency services and transportation to remote areas. Dental services, eye care, chiropractic, and other such related services could be offered through the universal regional system, but may be "farmed out" by the region. The bottom line is that no area in the nation would be without medical or related services because of lack of access to facilities. Regionalization could happen under a Social Capitalist economic system and control over capitalist greed.

6.4   Cost Containment

Nearly every hospital provides a full range of services, with much of the specialized equipment being unused much of the time. When this expensive equipment sits unused, it must still be paid for by some user of services. This tends to drive costs higher and higher since each facility is its own universe. Proper regionalization could implement efficiency that would drive costs down without hampering the provision of care.

The profits of doctors and companies that provide medical equipment and supplies must also be monitored and held to a reasonable level. Technological advancements cannot be stifled, but unreasonable profiteering must be controlled in the public interest. Again, the question must be asked if it is in the public interest to control medical costs, make medical care available to all, and keep the cost of health care reasonable. The answer is, clearly, yes! It would again be the responsibility of specialists in the area of medical services to audit the charges to ensure appropriateness and to eliminate profiteering. It is the responsibility of government to see that what is in the public interest is provided. If the medical industry cannot or will not provide for the medical needs of the public, for whatever reasons, then government must ensure that the public interest is provided for through controls, oversight, and auditing. An accountability system must be developed in which charges for services as provided by the regions and paid under a universal system are constantly reviewed by competent personnel for integrity in billing and appropriateness of charges.

In the final determination, through regionalization and by eliminating profiteering, duplication of coverages, and duplication of services, the costs to provide national health care would go down. In addition, by improving efficiency, auditing, and maintaining an incentive to contain costs, everyone could be provided complete health care coverage that would be affordable. However, in no event can the innovation and advancement that is characteristic of medical technology be hindered. The medical industry that provides a virtually uninhibited provision for research and development must not be hindered.

Cost containment must include pharmaceutical companies and prescription drugs. Cost containment is not accomplished by letting the greedy pharmaceutical and insurance companies write the programs that become law to ensure their profits. Deals must not be allowed to be made between the government and pharmaceutical companies that makes prescription drugs less expensive in other countries than in the United States of America. The manufacture of drugs by an American company that will cost more to purchase in the United States than in other countries just so the pharmaceutical companies can reap obscene profits will be illegal under Social Capitalism.

6.5   Health Insurance

Health insurance has evolved to the point that only the wealthy can afford it unless it is included as a benefit through employment. In addition, the selective nature of insurance underwriting excludes coverage for those who need it the most—those with prior conditions or a family history of medical problems. To add to these problems, there are a greater number of elderly citizens as a percent of the population every year, and they require a greater commitment of medical services. Because of this, there is no question about where the costs of insurance and medical care are headed.

The basic problem of affordable health care again is the result of the failure of the unfettered capitalist economic system to require the capitalists and employers to provide full employment at a living wage and benefits, including health care insurance. To compensate for the unfair economic system, employees turned to unions to negotiate greater equality in the workplace for the working class. Had the capitalist employers been required to provide a living wage, the working class employees could have afforded their own health care insurance. However, the greed of the capitalists and the desire to cut all costs in order to maximize obscene profits put the working class in the position of not enough income to afford health insurance.

Health insurance companies, and many insurance companies in general, are a classic example of unfettered capitalism at work. Insurance companies are extremely selective in whom and for what they will insure. This practice of selective underwriting by insurance companies alone is a significant statement for a universal health care system.

Profiteering through the unavailability or overpricing of health care, to the point of a lucrative lifestyle for some at the misery and expense of others, is not only illogical, but socially, morally, and ethically wrong.

The need for health insurance through insurance companies would still exist under a national health care system, but not to the degree currently in place. Other insurance coverages, such as life insurance, automobile, homeowners', businesses', etc., would continue to be necessary. The transition to a universal national system should not be a burden on most insurance companies as they have excluded millions from health care coverage already. Here again, the inherent greed of capitalists under unfettered capitalism rears its ugly head and must be regulated through Social Capitalism.

"A man willing to work, and unable to find work,
is perhaps the saddest sight that fortune's inequality
exhibits under the sun."
—Thomas Carlyle

"Not only our future economic soundness but the very
soundness of our democratic institutions depends on the
determination of our Government to give employment to
idle men."
—Franklin D. Roosevelt

7. Employment

The greatest asset in any company is the brains of its working class employees. Through the public education system, Americans have achieved an education with an ability to think and reason. Companies that do not involve their working class employees in production or service decisions will never maximize efficiency and productivity. Wise companies that don't pander to total capitalist greed do in fact get working class employees involved in company decisions. Most of these same companies have the other attributes desired by the working class and also have very little employment turnover. In addition, some companies are selling or reverting their interest in their company to their employees upon retirement of the original ownership/management. This employee ownership option is a strong indication of the recognition that working class employees can in fact operate a company without the need for a capitalist at the helm.

Having unemployed workers is a terrible waste of their education and productive ability. The answer to such a waste is a full employment policy at living wages and benefits in the private sector. When the nation has full employment, everyone wins; capitalists by increased profits, the working class through earning a living wage and benefits and having the ability to purchase to improve their standard of living, and government by increased tax revenue and a reduction in unemployment programs. The development of Social Capitalism could bring about such private sector full employment.

The greatest asset in any company is the brains of its employees. If those brains are not fully utilized through involvement in the company, the company will never maximize efficiency and productivity.

The government must pursue every option available in support of private and public sector jobs at a living wage and benefits for all of the employable working class. To start with, there must be a declared economic policy based on Social Capitalism. Then, enterprise zones, capital gains tax reductions on job-creating investments, investment tax credits for job-creating investments, employment tax credits, and buy-American incentives through a tax credit must all be implemented. None of these measures can be a stand-alone solution. Every measure conceivable must be utilized to create full employment. Enterprise zones that provide tax incentives to businesses for hiring and constructing in the zones for a minimum period of five to ten years will get people to work while saving taxpayer dollars. However, caution must be taken to ensure that the jobs are not simply from relocated companies for a greater profit motive. Retaining the capital gains tax only on investments that create jobs will provide the incentive for private sector investment in job creation. Tax credits for investments that create jobs will provide an incentive that will result not only in substantial job creation at the user end, but also at the point that the equipment or other property is constructed. Taxation of the private sector and then providing tax credits based on the degree of employment provided will induce employment. To buy American-made products is to provide an incentive to purchase products made in and by Americans, thus creating and retaining jobs. Every one of these measures will provide tremendous benefits to the working class.

In addition, to support businesses in the creation of jobs, government cannot continue to harbor the incompetent. Wages and salaries are earned, not paid out for showing up. To the same end, unions, as the agents of employees, must work with government to ensure that union requests for members do not diminish the productivity effort. Other employment must be found for those displaced by technology. Retraining or relocation must take priority over lack of productivity. Avenues must be pursued that will result in the upholding of commitments or contracts so all sides are treated fairly. The practice of retaining people in jobs in defense or the military as "make-work" jobs simply because to dismiss them would put the individual out of work must be eliminated. It is undesirable to retain a position that is no longer needed simply to provide a paycheck. Retaining people in obsolete government positions to give them a paycheck and keep them off unemployment or welfare is also undesirable. Providing every opportunity and incentive to the private and public sectors to create and retain jobs is preferred. A three-party partnership with a full employment opportunity policy, as with Social Capitalism, is desirable.

It should be obvious that government must do everything within its power to promote job creation in the private and public sectors. Is this the case currently? No, but it must become the point of emphasis!

Inefficient government employees perpetuates inefficiency in government. When employees see one person getting by without providing optimum productivity, the message is sent to other employees that inefficiency is tolerated. No inefficiency in the administration of tax dollars should be tolerated. Government, in the interest of the working class and as the trustee of the taxpayers, must maximize efficiency in the public sector just as in the private sector. It is not efficient to spend millions on spare military parts for equipment that is retired or no longer needed. It is not efficient to provide programs without the regulatory oversight and agents to ensure efficiency. It is not efficient to spend billions on foreign aid without assurances that the funds are being administered to help the people as intended. The list of inefficiencies goes on and on. Government-funded inspectors must be put in place by regulation to oversee productivity and to temper greed. Once a full employment policy and the corresponding incentives are in place, the unnecessary and wasteful government positions could be eliminated. There will, however, always be a need for some social programs, like unemployment for the temporarily unemployed and welfare for the unemployable.

The democratic way should be to provide for those less fortunate; and, indeed, the essence of life is for everyone to make the best they can of life with what they have, while at the same time making life better for the less fortunate. The same applies to government and capitalists, where the effort must be to do the best they can for the working class. Capitalist greed, perpetuated by government's blind faith in unfettered capitalism, is the enemy of prosperity for all. To provide for the working class, there must be work, jobs, and full employment opportunities. This can be accomplished through a Social Capitalist economic system in which there is a three-party partnership to maximize the economy.

The perception that the public and private sectors cannot provide full employment at a living wage is incorrect under existing unfettered capitalism economic thinking, which must be changed.

A policy of full employment at a living wage and benefits need not be seen as detrimental to the business sector when coupled with associated policies. The solution to employment problems is not singular, but plural. To ensure that businesses can fully employ the entire work force at a living wage, there must also be job creation incentives. A policy of full employment through a rethinking of economic values is in keeping with a Social Capitalist economic system. A policy of full employment will result in the reduction or elimination of numerous other associated social problems. A compassionate government administration would find any degree of unemployment intolerable. How can an administration get excited over a reduction in the number of people filing for unemployment benefits in any given month when the government policy should be full employment? If a policy of full employment existed, the excitement would be over the number of positions and job openings that are filled.

It is not the cost to employ a person that should concern the government or capitalists, but rather the cost to a family and society not to employ.

There is no shame in being rich or privileged. There are few if any Americans who would not choose to be rich. The impetus must be on providing the opportunity for all of the working class to be some degree of "rich" through employment at a living wage and benefits. This can be done only if the opportunity for employment is available to all of the working class, no matter where they may live. Government must align with businesses and capitalists and the working class to ensure that every able-bodied member of the working class has a job under a Social Capitalist economic system.

An argument can be made that the very wealth that capitalists would exploit was accumulated by overcharging the less fortunate, which contributes to their less than desirable lifestyle. Although the rule in an unfettered capitalism economic system is that the provider may charge whatever the market will bear, this does not mutually make it right to overcharge or charge the maximum that the market will bear. Such tactics, without reciprocity to those who provided such wealth, are another reason there is a constant perception that the rich get richer while the poor get poorer. It is time for a rethinking of values to replace greed with compassion and social responsibility. If this is done, many more of the working class can achieve the dreams that are possible only in a democracy.

It is a sad day for democracy when the policies of the government are manipulated into making the rich richer and the poor poorer, and pit capitalists against the working class. What could be worse than having to import all the electronics sold in a democratic nation? What could be worse than automobile manufacturers moving out of a democratic nation and taking working class jobs with them? What could be worse than having over 50 percent of a nation's energy imported, including the jobs that produce that energy? What could be worse than a government of the capitalist, by the capitalist, and for the capitalist, with policies based on capitalist profits and reduced taxes and not on the needs of the working class? These problems and situations are caused by the failure of government to distinguish and adopt a distinct economic policy. Social Capitalism with a full employment policy and a declaration of social equality in economic opportunity must be adopted by any democratic nation.

7.1 Full Employment Policy

Without doubt, the greatest avenue of approach to the best that a democratic nation can be is the opportunity of employment for every able-bodied adult. It is jobs for the working class that fuel and turn the wheels of an economy. A democracy can have all the ideas and inventions that can be imagined, but if they do not result in jobs, dependence on the government grows. Sadly, though, the government is without a visible means of support except for taxation. People can't pay taxes if people do not have jobs. Government must support every possible effort that will assist or induce private sector businesses in creating the opportunity for employment at a living wage for the working class. Businesses, to compete in a global economy, must involve employees in the business process to the degree that employees are proud and fairly compensated. The means to accomplish this partnership for economic and social prosperity is a Social Capitalist economic system. A democratic nation can no longer operate with only the flawed definition of unfettered capitalism as a guide. Without a declared economic policy, it is the same as trying to operate a democratic government with only the definition of democracy as a guide instead of the US Constitution.

The days in a democracy with unfettered capitalism and the "I've got mine and to heck with everyone else" attitude must give way to a democracy with a Social Capitalist economic system in which equality in opportunity and economic cooperation are combined to maximize efficiency and output.

With a full employment policy at a living wage and benefits, employment incentives to the private sector, and taxation based on employment, small and medium-sized businesses would flourish throughout the nation. The ideal private sector structure is a strong small business sector where employment, social responsibility, and employer/employee partnerships are the standard. The days of conglomerates buying up everything in sight for a profit motive must be the exception and not the rule. Businesses and individual capitalists, whose only purpose is to amass dollars without appropriate levels of employment and social responsibility, must be taxed accordingly or broken up in favor of businesses that employ.

Working class Americans think they have equal economic opportunity under unfettered capitalism, but many are underemployed, unemployed, homeless, and on social programs for lack of equal employment opportunity at a living wage.

There can be a three-party partnership in the economic system, and it can lead to prosperity. However, it will not happen without a change in the leadership of a nation to recognize and support equal rights and opportunities for all. Business and government have a responsibility to provide equal opportunity for the working class. Nothing short of equality and a full employment policy will provide for the future, and only the voters in a democracy can make it happen.

Economists may state that full employment is counterproductive and will result in the employees being able to dictate wages to businesses that won't be able to replace disenchanted employees. This is because it is falsely perceived that if full employment were ever achieved, then labor, not management and ownership, would dictate wages. They assert this will result in employers having to pay higher wages, probably even to the point of a living wage and benefits, and in their businesses losing their profitability. This would be true if a full employment policy were not coupled with additional measures to ensure full employment, such as a buy-American policy, employment tax credits, and government loan guarantees to viable potential business entities. It is the capitalist ideal that owners, not labor, determine and dictate what is best for labor, and labor should be satisfied with what is dictated. This ideal is perpetuated by having a continuous supply of unemployed workers. Then ownership and management can always challenge the cry of the working class for higher wages by a reminder that there are always other unemployed workers available as replacements. Unemployment is in the interest of the wealthy that derive their wealth from the labor of others, for which they may pay less than a living wage and provide less than full employment. This ideal is not in the interest of the working class. Therefore, unemployment must be eliminated in favor of a government full employment policy under a Social Capitalist economic system.

There is an annual insertion into the economy of thousands of newly educated individuals. In addition, there is a wide range of employment levels, as determined by the range in wages and salaries paid. Therefore, there would be a continual upward mobility from less technical jobs to more technical jobs. At the other end, there is a large group of experienced, semiretired people who can provide additional assurances of available labor. This ensures a continual supply to the labor force, which includes a certain level of unemployment. This should provide ample protection from attaining the goal of full employment, but should not detract from a full employment policy. Since the government guarantees taxation of citizens, the government must guarantee the opportunity to be gainfully employed to be able to pay the taxes.

There are people who are very concerned about the rich becoming richer if the government acts to create incentives that will lead to job creation. There are even those who question whether certain actions by the government will even create jobs. These people must understand "it doesn't matter!" Every effort and facility available to the government that has even the potential for job creation must be enacted without regard for who is perceived as profiting from the action. This country was founded on the premise that if you work hard, you can profit from your work. If people have no work, the entire premise is lost, and the democracy falls deeper and deeper into an unequal state.

> *It must be recognized that the long-term suffering of the working class caused by unemployment must be addressed at any cost with a full employment policy, lest additional generations are lost to an economic system of unequal opportunity.*

Jobs for every able-bodied member of a democracy are the means by which past wrongs may be set right. Some would state that the government is not in the business of creating jobs, and this is true in most cases. Therefore, it is the responsibility of government to provide the incentives to the private sector for job creation which will reduce dependency on taxpayers. In addition, it is the responsibility of government to create job opportunities in areas of infrastructure improvement and government services that are not undertaken by the private sector. Only through government incentives will individuals and businesses relinquish funds from safe harbors to invest and take risks to increase the number of jobs. As jobs are created, and individuals are moved from unemployment to the productivity of the private or public sectors, the tax base increases, and a greater fairness and equality are achieved.

In the quest for equal economic opportunity in a civilized society, it is not only the monetary savings to the taxpayer that is important in developing gainful employment. The children of a family begin to learn that there is hope through opportunity for earning a living and a better way of life. With an income, the family will move from subsidized housing to the private sector as a renter or home buyer. There will be an upgraded automobile or consumer purchases that would be otherwise unavailable. Additional people need to be employed to produce the housing, automobiles, and consumer products that will be purchased. In addition, people will have to be employed to provide the equipment and facilities that will be invested in by the private sector. The family will pay taxes and become productive members of society, producing an additional inflow of funds to the government coffers. Hopelessness would be replaced with hope and opportunity, and crime would diminish. With the added incentive of a buy-American program, there is greater assurance of job creation. These and many more are the benefits of a full employment policy under a Social Capitalist economic system.

Children of unemployed families can have low self-esteem and be less than enthusiastic about their futures and in some cases revert to the perceived quick profits of crime.

Voters should be aware that expansion of the tax base is absolutely necessary for the survival of a democratic way of life. They must not be misled by greedy capitalists that will expound the simple and reject or degrade the difficult as being unworkable as they accumulate their profits and wealth from an unfair economic system. A working class government managed by statesmen and stateswomen with integrity and business sense would realize the benefits of full employment at living wages and the resulting maximized tax base. They would recognize Social Capitalism and full employment as solutions and not as quick fixes to fiscal and economic policy.

Full employment is so vital to the economy of a democracy that if the private sector cannot or will not create the jobs needed for full employment, then the government must tax the wealth and use the tax funds to create government programs to effect full employment at a living wage and benefits. This practice worked after the Great Depression and can work again even better given that prior experience. The wealth of a nation must be utilized for the betterment of all in a democratic nation, not just the greedy few.

7.2   Living Wage

A government policy of full employment would be contrary to the corporate business interest of controlling the wage structure of employees by having an available supply of the unemployed. The closer to full employment that a nation gets, the greater the ability of the wage earner to achieve a living wage. What is wrong with ensuring that the working class in a democracy, who have only their labor to sell, receive a living wage for their work? Why, then, in a democracy should there be such disparity between the "haves" and the "have-nots?" The owners of the means of production and distribution, the capitalist elite, are virtually guaranteed a living wage through their ownership. Why, then, doesn't the economic system that would purport equity under democracy not also provide for equal economic opportunity? Isn't providing a living wage to the working class very much in keeping with the essence of life, which is to do the best one can while also providing for others? Democracy and the working class need the equity that would be provided under an adopted Social Capitalist economic system.

A full employment policy must include provision for a living wage and living benefits. Those who may respond that "businesses can't possibly provide a guaranteed living wage for fear of bankruptcy" are too quick to jump to conclusions. Capitalist companies spend millions on advertising and promoting sporting events or any other activity they may rationalize, but when it comes to ensuring a living wage for employees, they claim there is no money. Companies scream that they will have to lay off employees if the minimum wage is changed to a living wage, but they pay stockholders and corporate executives millions in salaries and bonuses. The wealthy have enough money to drive the stock market to unforeseen highs while working class wages are dropping and unemployment is increasing. If the private sector won't voluntarily pay a living wage, then government tax policy and minimum wage laws must do it for them. The wealth in America indicates that it is time that all Americans are provided a guaranteed living wage, and a guaranteed opportunity to participate in the American dream. The minimum wage laws must become the "living wage and benefits laws." The government must look out for the majority, the working class, and not succumb to threats to lay off employees if wages are increased. Innovative ideas must be offered that will result in full employment at living wages. Why couldn't there be a living wage for high school graduates and a somewhat lower living wage for those who drop out? Wouldn't the benefits of such an incentive to complete high school provide a substantial return to the working class over the lifetime of the graduates versus nongraduates?

What is the dream of democracy to the vast numbers of the unemployed and out of work, including those on social programs? What is the dream of democracy to minorities, whose unemployment and perceived dependence on taxpayers are as much a stigma for discrimination and racism as color or religion? The dream of democracy is to have the freedom and opportunity to be the best one can be in a society free from the ills found in other societies. The dream can only become reality if the basis for attaining the dream is available to everyone. That basis is gainful employment at a living wage and benefits under a Social Capitalist economic system. Companies that threaten to eliminate jobs if wages are increased will be replaced by those companies that will emerge under Social Capitalism and equal economic opportunity policies. The intelligence and entrepreneurship of the working class will, with the proper economic policies in place, ensure ample employment opportunities for all in a democracy.

7.3   Employment Incentives

Businesses, in return for the wealth that is provided to them through the policies of a Social Capitalist economic system, must have a responsibility to the working class and society that provided the opportunity for their wealth in the first place. Capitalist and corporate businesses must be taxed to the point that all the working class are either employed or provided for. Government must provide the policies, incentives, tax credits, or employment rebates that businesses need to provide employment opportunity for all. To accomplish this, a democracy does not need a two-partner— government and capitalist—economic relationship; it needs a three-partner relationship—working class, government, and capitalist— under a Social Capitalist economic system.

There is no logical argument that would justify multimillion-dollar salaries and bonuses to corporate executives. The rationale for such exorbitant salaries is that nothing is wrong with it under the unfettered capitalist economic system. This rationale is wrong. Under a Social Capitalist economic system which would include social responsibility, such expenditures would be grossly unjust. Therefore, the only explanation is greed. In other words, wealth for the sake of wealth is greed. Wealth for the sake of helping others, including employees, is compassion. Many capitalists would rather be remembered as compassionate, but most are primarily motivated by greed. Elite capitalists, in general, recognize there should be a social responsibility that goes along with their accumulation of wealth. However, capitalists aren't about to bring it up as long as the economic system is rigged in their favor and doesn't require them to adhere to a social responsibility as would be required under a Social Capitalist economic system.

In return for the inducements that must be offered by government to businesses or for the creation of businesses that will provide the opportunity for employment to all, the businesses must accept a responsibility. It is time for businesses in the greatest nation on earth to acknowledge that their employees are a major factor in their businesses. There is nothing wrong with a business making a profit for those who put up the investment that created the business and the jobs for the employees. However, that profit must not be at the expense of employees.

Job creation incentives provide long-term results that are much greater than the incentives offered. The government wins, the individuals win, and businesses win, while the economy flourishes. The benefits of job creation should not be influenced by the concern of some that the rich may get richer from such incentives. Of course the rich will gain from the creation of jobs. Isn't that the nature of a capitalist economy? It should not be the intent of the federal government, the economic system, or any other level of government to diminish the ranks of the rich. Rather, the emphasis must be to diminish the ranks of the poor by providing incentives to induce those who have flourished to invest and employ those who have not. It must be the intent of government and capitalists to work in an economic partnership with the working class, not as adversaries.

A reasonable financial policy that makes financing available for business expansion and startups can create jobs. A greater emphasis on business education and involvement by the private sector in the classroom can create jobs. A reduction in the regulation of business in areas that do not affect the public health and safety or public interest can create jobs. A full employment policy by the government that provides incentives to businesses for employment and net new job creation will provide jobs. A government guaranteed loan policy that is based on the profit potential of the venture as opposed to requiring 100 percent collateral will create jobs. Investing in a buy-American policy, as opposed to foreign trade agreements and foreign aid giveaway programs, will create jobs. The major emphasis of the government must be on job creation and employment in the private and public sectors, and anything short of that is inadequate. Those who do not put an emphasis on job creation are the greedy capitalists including those who move jobs out of the country for greater profits.

It is true that America still has open competition in the marketplace. It is also true that the means of production and distribution are privately or corporately owned. It is no longer true that development is proportionate to the increasing accumulation and reinvestment of profits. Profits are accumulated but they are not being reinvested proportionately in new development or expansion that creates jobs. The current policies of the government do not promote the investment of profits in development, expansion, and jobs. When the Reaganomics tax cuts for the wealthy took place in the 1980s, the stock market went to new all-time highs and has even gone higher with the tax cuts for the wealthy since 2000. If those tax cuts had been invested into job creation, there would be full employment today. Knowing now that tax cuts for the wealthy do not lead to job creation, but rather to hoarding wealth in offshore tax shelters to enhance capitalist profits, the answer is clear. The tax cuts for the wealthy must be rolled back under a Social Capitalist economic system.

Unfettered capitalism must be replaced with Social Capitalism. It must also be the policy of government, in the interest of the working class, to provide the incentives that will induce investment of profits in development and jobs, not in offshore tax shelters. If stock market investing were the proper method of providing development and jobs, why then is there not full employment and a flourishing economy when the stock market soars to record highs? Because stock market investing isn't the best method of creating or developing jobs! If lowering interest rates resulted in business expansion and higher employment, why isn't there full employment and a healthy economy when interest rates drop from 11 percent to 4 percent, or lower? Because lowering interest rates does not, in and of itself, result in business expansion and job creation! The major action/reaction that is created by movement in the stock market or interest rates is between these two investment markets and the capitalist individuals who play those markets. How many times has the speculation of capitalists raised havoc on the financial markets through capitalist speculation and trading using leveraging? It happened with the Great Depression, it happened with the savings-and-loan bailout, and it's happening again with the bailout of too-big-to-fail banks. The stock markets, hedge funds, derivatives, commodities markets, and speculation on land and mortgages are casinos for the capitalists in which the working class provide and lose their meager dollars to finance the games of the capitalists. When these casinos do get into trouble or fail, the perpetrators cry to the government for a bailout, and the taxpayers are shafted again. In a democracy, these practices and markets must be regulated by government under a Social Capitalist economic system to control the greed of capitalists and protect taxpayers.

Jobs are created by the private sector as a direct result of the benefit to be gained by providing the jobs. If there are few incentives to expand, develop, or create new jobs, profits will be invested elsewhere to gain the highest return. The government must recognize this and provide the job creation incentives to the private sector that will result in expansion, new development, and job creation. The ill-conceived tax reform act of 1986 virtually eliminated any job creation incentives that were in place in America. It is exactly the wrong policy to believe that the way to provide job creation incentives to the private sector is to provide tax cuts for the rich. Those who would not support job creation incentives do not fully understand what is in the best interest of the working class, or they are profiting handsomely by the current unfettered capitalist economic policy.

Americans have a choice: to support politicians who create tax policy that is antiworking class, antijobs, pro-corporate subsidies and unreasonable capitalist profits; or, to support working class statesmen and stateswomen in government who will create employment policies and incentives that will put people to work, decrease unemployment, increase the number of taxpayers, and reduce the tax burden on everyone. The question should be, what does the government have to put in place to create the jobs that will get the economy going and keep it going for everyone? The answer is found in a Social Capitalist economic system.

Well-paying jobs make a strong economy by providing the working class spending power and a tax base that in turn provides more jobs. With higher tax rates on those that do not employ under Social Capitalism and government regulation, job creation will be the most desirable alternative to capitalists over higher taxes and hoarding of profits. Job creation incentives can be in any number of forms, any or all of which must be considered to put a country into a strong economy. The creation of jobs must also have a higher priority than the federal deficit or the national debt, but only in the short term. Once full employment is achieved, the increased tax base would mutually begin a reduction in the federal deficit and national debt. With full employment plans could begin for any further reductions in the annual deficit and national debt.

Enterprise zones are needed that will create jobs in areas that are less attractive or rural by giving business the incentives to locate in these areas of high unemployment. A buy-American tax credit or rebate program that will provide for employment in the manufacture of products made in America will create new jobs and keep jobs from being moved out of the country. The buy-American policy will also ensure that taxes on products sold in America will be paid in America, not circumvented by importing companies. Employment tax credits are needed to employ all able-bodied Americans, including the economically disadvantaged. Investment credits must be revisited as an incentive to purchase equipment and build plants, which will not only create jobs in the plants and in using the equipment, but also in the construction of the buildings and equipment. Taxes on capital gains that result in job creation must be structured to be an incentive to invest in job creation, rather than putting funds into the safe haven of interest-bearing, government-backed accounts or offshore accounts. A government loan guarantee program would ensure that all viable job creation and employment opportunities by entrepreneurs (job creators) are not rejected for lack of funding. Businesses must be encouraged through incentives to provide apprenticeship and training programs that will lead to full-time gainful employment for those who would otherwise be unemployable. There may be any number of additional options and incentives that can be explored or implemented to create jobs. People should be encouraged to step forward with their ideas on job creation, and on any other matters of concern. Policies generated by the government from these ideas must support job creation and investment in job creation under Social Capitalism.

All of these incentives will bring back the employment that is needed to provide the economic base that will offset the spending policies now in place. The cycle must begin with government providing business with incentives to promote job creation. In turn, businesses create net new jobs that put the unemployed to work at a living wage and benefits, the working class contribute to a tax base that is necessary to run the country, and the taxes provide the incentives to businesses to keep employment up, as well as providing for other government programs. The only link in this cycle that creates the opportunity for the rest of the cycle to work is employment and job creation. Without employment and job creation, the cycle is short-circuited and those who do work have to pay for those who don't.

Job creation incentives, while of the greatest importance to the existence of an economic system, are also the cheapest means available with which to attack stagnation and a slow economy. Even if all the incentives are set in place, the additional cost to the taxpayers is effectively zero. If the unemployed become employed because of the incentives, the cost of their support, social services, or unemployment tax dollars now goes to support the incentives, instead of supporting the unemployed. From here, everything else works. Beyond the initial incentives, there is virtually no additional expenditure of tax dollars on those employed. In fact, they are now taxpayers, not tax dollar users. The key to the incentive programs is net new jobs created and an economic system of Social Capitalism. Free trade agreements like NAFTA, CAFTA, and other "free" trade agreements that are set in place for greater capitalist profits are not employment incentives to the working class; they are disincentives and should be rescinded in favor of fair trade agreements. Fair trade agreements would include the working class and not just capitalist greed as a factor in the agreement.

There are those who have the power to effect legislation that will put all of the working class to work but who have chosen not to provide that impetus. Some have even chosen to discourage any such impetus, under the belief that to do so will only make the rich richer and the poor poorer. Under capitalism, the only hope for minorities and the less fortunate is jobs. How can the poor be poorer if they go from unemployed to employed at a living wage? How can inducing those with money to put it into job creation instead of into the stock market or interest-bearing accounts make any difference in the wealth they will accumulate? Those who say that offering incentives to businesses to create jobs will only benefit the rich and increase the federal deficit are wrong. How can a provision for incentives to businesses to hire people increase the deficit when those to be employed are not working anyway?

7.4 Employment Tax Credits

Employment tax credits have been around for quite some time as an incentive to employ minorities and the disadvantaged. As a part of Social Capitalism and a full employment policy, the credit should be extended to any employment, regardless of circumstance, together with substantially higher taxes on the capitalists and corporations. An employment tax credit, coupled with significantly higher taxes on the wealthy, would be the means for businesses with significant employment to recoup their profits through employment tax credits. Employment tax credits would reward businesses that employ and penalize businesses or wealthy individuals that don't employ. The higher taxes would be a control over capitalist greed while still allowing the capitalists to profit from their ventures.

For example, a business that employed one hundred people would pay taxes at 75 percent of, say, a $1,000,000 taxable income, resulting in a tax bill of $750,000 (compared to current taxes of, say, $330,000). But because the business has one hundred employees and is paying a living wage and benefits, the business would receive an employment tax credit off the $750,000 tax bill of $4,500 per employee, or $450,000. The resulting $300,000 tax bill is actually a net tax savings or additional profit to the business of $30,000 ($330,000 – $300,000). A business or individual that made such huge profits but did not employ would pay the full $750,000 in taxes.

7.5   Employees

Unfettered capitalism expounds that those that own and distribute will provide jobs for the rest if they so choose and at the wages they choose to pay. The "I will do this for employees if I so choose" must become "We, as a company, as an industry, as the capitalists, will do this for the working class and thereby for the nation." This can only happen through an association of equals, not adversaries. The adversarial relationship between capitalists, the working class, and government must end. The economic relationship must become the three-party partnership, not unfettered capitalism as usual. The capitalists must own up to their social responsibility under the system that provided for their success by the effort of many others. However, this owning up does not mean the elimination of capitalism, but rather that true fairness in the economy be recognized under democracy and Social Capitalism as what was intended.

In a democracy, virtually every individual is now educated and wants to be proud of where he or she works. People want to be able to go home to their children and spouse and say they are happy and proud they work for a good company. Children want to be proud and brag about where their parents work, but how can they if their parents are not respected or content with their employment? Every worker from a custodian to a line worker to an executive would like to be able to be proud. With a Social Capitalist economic system, being able to be proud of where one works can become a reality.

Employees want to be proud of where they work, but often pride is not possible because of the lack of a living wage, lack of respect from management or owners, or lack of active participation in the business while the company and owner/stockholders prosper.

It is up to the owners and managers, the capitalists, to make it happen. Owners and managers must involve their employees in operating the business at every opportunity possible. This could involve taking and considering suggestions, or putting representatives from the ranks of employees into the decision-making process. It is human nature to strive to do one's best. However, if employees are asked to do something that they know could be done better, they are being asked to do less than their best which can lead to discontent and reduced productivity. These concerns must be responded to through involvement in the process. There must be a partnership between owners/managers and labor, not an adversarial relationship. Proud and involved employees are productive employees. Proud, involved, and productive employees can be efficient employees, if the owners and management let it happen.

With a flawed unfettered capitalist economic system, many employees simply are earning a living as opposed to enjoying a career. A change to a Social Capitalist economic system can change the relationship between owners and employees.

In business as in every aspect of life in a democracy, respect is earned, not commanded. The involvement of employees shows respect for their intelligence and the contributions they make to the company.

This in turn earns their respect for the company, which translates into proud employees. In addition, those who work with the products of a company on a daily basis can offer ideas on possible improvements that will increase quality, productivity, and efficiency. The more minds put to use in quest of a single goal, as in producing a product, the better that product can be in competition for a market share, especially in a global economy. When products have a guaranteed market, the need for this efficiency and involvement is reduced because inefficiency can be made up by an increased asking price. However, as competition increases, quality and efficiency must increase and, indeed, be maximized to retain a market share or to be the market leader.

Proof of the need for or success of a three-partner relationship with proud and productive employees is already evident through those few companies in America that have recognized and pursued such a partnership between management and labor. In reports these companies have already made, employees would have it no other way, management as an equal partner is pleased, and the businesses are successful. What else need be said!

Under democracy and a Social Capitalist economic system, every employee deserves the right to be proud of their employment, and it is the responsibility of the public or private sector employers to make it possible.

A Social Capitalist economic system will provide everyone the opportunity for a piece of the capitalist system. Businesses, in return for the right to own the means of production and distribution, must share the wealth generated by such ownership with those who make it possible, their employees. The government provides for private ownership through capitalism, which in turn is supposed to provide jobs for all the rest of the people. The flaws in the system have allowed the capitalist owners to avoid the responsibility of providing for the working class. The government has responded with social programs, which the capitalists dislike and want to eliminate.

A Social Capitalist economic policy that would provide for a three-party partnership is the means by which democracy will survive. America no longer has a lock on specific markets or economic institutions. America is an economic player just like other nations. Previously, competition between companies in America was to capture American markets; now the emphasis must be on America as a nation competing for greater markets, but not at the expense of the American working class through harmful trade agreements. Unfettered capitalism expounds that those that own and distribute will provide jobs for the rest if they so choose and at the wages they choose to pay. However, government has had to invoke minimum wage laws as an attempt to control capitalist greed.

7.6   Unions

The government controls taxation and the money supply in America, therefore the interests of government are well protected. Businesses generally have the capital to secure whatever services may be needed to operate their businesses effectively, and therefore their interests are protected. Employees—the working class—on the other hand, having no resources and only their labor to sell, have been classically left to fend for themselves or become capitalists from nothing. For many reasons, some more obvious than others, labor unions evolved as the agents for labor. Unfortunately, capitalists had already determined that they had every right to exploit, control, and dictate to labor whatever they pleased in return for providing jobs. Additionally, businesses fully expected, under the limited and self-serving application of unfettered capitalism, that employees should take it or leave it but had no right to organize. Labor is led to believe they have no right to make demands on the capitalists, who are simply following the prescribed unfettered capitalist economic system that lets capitalists do as they please with labor. In keeping with controlling capitalist greed, unions must not only be allowed but also have government protection under a Social Capitalist economic system. However, even under a Social Capitalist economic system, unions will still be needed as a government control over greed to get the best possible employment contract for union members.

Unions as agents of the working class are as logical within an economic system in which the working class sells its labor as agents are within the government and private sector to ensure the best return on their investments.

Reality has proven that labor has every right to participate as a full partner in a democratic economy. A democratic economy must be three sided, not two sided with some leftovers. The organization of labor through unions, or some other organization, is in keeping with the real economic structure in a democracy and in keeping with the practice of being allowed to be represented by agents. Sports figures have agents who will uphold and secure the best possible benefits for their clients. Governments have agencies that try to ensure that the taxpayers are getting the best benefit from their tax dollars. Businesses have agents that ensure they maximize profits from the products they produce and distribute. Why, then, shouldn't the working class in a capitalist democracy, who have only their labor to sell to earn a living, have an agent such as unions to ensure the best possible benefit from their labor? It is totally logical and long overdue that unions must be recognized as a legitimate right of the working class.

Even with unions, employees—and, in fact, all wage earners—must also remember that a wage is earned, not given out for showing up. To some, the security a union has provided means that they can do less and get paid more. This is wrong. Unions are to provide for the best possible standard of living for their members, but they must also ensure that a paycheck is earned. If it were not for unions in America, it is likely that the working class would still be working six or seven days a week and ten or more hours a day. Working conditions and child labor would be much worse than today.

Workers cannot be blamed for organizing and/or belonging to unions that would try to improve their standard of living. Unions are a natural reaction to an unfettered capitalist economic system. Unions evolved because owners and managers did not treat employees with the respect necessary to allow them to be proud of their work and earn a living wage and benefits. Worker discontent breeds change, and the change was to unionize. However, unions need not be an obstacle to decisions by owners and management to provide a work environment in which their employees can be proud. Involvement of employees, whether unionized or not, leads to enhanced productivity and efficiency. Unions are a result of the failure to establish a Social Capitalist economic system.

An argument can be made that unions are a direct result of the lack of a complete definition of capitalism and a declared equal opportunity economic policy. Had there been Social Capitalism, in which the social responsibility was delegated to capitalists, there would not have been a need for the working class to organize under unions. Unions are the result of greedy capitalism, which capitalists have brought upon themselves. The working class would have been a partner in the economy, paid a living wage, and fully provided for by capitalists. There wouldn't have been a need for as many social programs associated with unfettered capitalism.

> *"We demand that big business give people a square deal."*
> —Theodore Roosevelt

The adversarial relationship between business and labor would not persist under Social Capitalism. It is obvious that the relationship is adversarial as evidenced by the give and take between unions and owners in recent years. When the unions negotiate for adequate wages and management complies, during good times everything is fine. However, when there is a downturn in the economy, one of the first requests by management is for concessions from the unions. This is characteristic of an adversarial relationship and not an association or partnership for a common purpose.

Greedy capitalists want to break unions, especially their role in support of political candidates that support the working class. This is an ironic twist that unions are not to be allowed to support candidates while the capitalists and their corporations can contribute virtually any amount of money to buy a political candidate. How is the voice of the working class to be heard in politics? The capitalists do not want the working class to be heard. It's as if by silencing the working class, the capitalists can cut costs and increase profits even further by exploitation and intimidation of the working class.

Under Social Capitalism, wages, salaries, benefits, and profits could be tied to performance and production even with union contracts representing employees. As the company and economy went, so would go the partnership, with both labor and management/owners benefiting or conceding as equals. Executive salaries, owner profits, and working class wages are all tied to the performance of the company in a responsible manner. Of course, those who take the risk to operate the venture must be rewarded, but that reward need not be at the expense of the working class. All aspects of a company would benefit from a degree of equality. There is nothing wrong with acquiring wealth as long as those who helped make it possible are not walked on, but walked with and provided for in the process.

7.7   Child Care

Unfettered capitalism and the failed policies of the government have often required that both parents of a family be employed to maintain a decent standard of living. Government policies that did not provide for a living wage, spending policies that exceeded revenues collected, capitalist greed, war, and an energy crisis have all contributed to the need for two-income families. From here, the issue arises of whether or not the government should provide day care for the children of working parents. The government should not provide day care, but the government should see that day care is provided through and sponsored by the private sector, whenever possible. If welfare is out and employment is in, then incentives to businesses, if necessary, to provide day care should be a standard under Social Capitalism.

Economic conditions have necessitated two-income families, and therefore there must be a provision for child care to be provided by the private sector, with government oversight and monitoring.

"A teacher affects eternity."

—Henry B. Adams

8. Education

There is no question that the opportunity for education has positively impacted the standard of living in a democracy. Education must be dynamic so that as new concepts or patterns emerge, education will change to meet and keep up with changing times. The days of reading, writing, and arithmetic, although still vital to the education of students, must be supplemented with the educational needs of a new century.

> *Education must not just teach literacy in order for students to participate in society as an equal; it must also teach critical thinking in order to be involved in the continual dynamic changes of society.*

When the norm in a country was an illiterate majority, the push for every citizen to become accomplished in reading, writing, and arithmetic was a noble effort that provided outstanding results. This was fine for an agricultural and industrial based economy, but that is no longer the norm. The current economy is business, service, computer, and technology based, and moving rapidly into the next generation, whatever that will be. The education system needs to prepare students for the business and economic world that exists today and will exist in the future.

There is diminishing opportunity for unskilled labor in a technologically advancing economy. It is time for greater involvement in education. In a Social Capitalist economic system, this would not only include teachers, administrators, and students, but also businesses and industries. Students must be motivated to learn, not just to attend school because it's the social requirement. What is wrong with specialized education? Why shouldn't students be exposed to career opportunities in high school or trade schools and allowed to pursue a specialty career? Some students cannot make it in high school or college, but may have other attributes which could be developed into trades with help from industry. Such an opportunity would be provided within a Social Capitalist economic system.

A Social Capitalist economic system would provide for the private sector to consider the recruitment of students (as in sports) for employment after graduation and upon attaining certain skills.

A plan is needed that will place the educational system on track to provide the business and professional leaders of tomorrow. It must provide all students the greatest opportunity for maximizing their education, not just getting an education. Education must be made interesting, and there must be an emphasis on the opportunities that abound for the educated student. Too many students graduate from school without really knowing what their options are. Field trips and seminars from industry and business must be brought together with videos on the various types of employment opportunities available to give students a sense of opportunity. This may be done early in high school and continued throughout a student's education. Colleges must incorporate on-the-job training into curriculums, in cooperation with businesses, as with student teaching, so students may learn early in their studies exactly what is expected on-the-job. The educational systems and parents must realize that students are constantly learning and developing throughout their formative years. Learning is not just taking place while in school, but at home, on the streets, in peer groups, and elsewhere.

The public education system that has gotten this far must be upheld and expanded, especially the infrastructure. In a Social Capitalism economic system, public education must be the rule and not privatization of education to allow capitalists to siphon off exorbitant profits from taxpayers under the pretense of educating students. The privatization of the education system is absolutely in keeping with unfettered capitalism, which is to diminish government and let capitalists run everything to obtain obscene tax payer profits to add to their accumulated wealth. In the meantime, education of students and the upkeep of public educational infrastructure must not be secondary to profits of capitalists. Once it is figured out that private education has suffered significantly under privatization, these capitalists will request a government bailout at additional taxpayer expense. A Social Capitalist economic system would support and enhance public education.

8.1   Motivation in Education

In education many students must be motivated to learn. The tendency is to "have to go to school," not "to learn." A possible motivating factor, under a full employment economic system, could be for businesses to seek and recruit students. Recruitments could be through the schools or teen centers. Recruited students, upon attaining a certain goal in their education, would be guaranteed a job with the recruiting business. Motivation would result and businesses would be conveying their needs to the educational system. For the disadvantaged and minorities, this method would instill hope and opportunity. Students must be motivated to stay in school and learn marketable skills.

America must recognize the high cost that the uneducated and undereducated will have on society and ensure through incentives that education and learning have the highest priority.

Incentives to students could provide the motivation necessary to encourage a reasonable effort in school. What is wrong with providing a guaranteed job through government or business incentives to students upon graduating from school and meeting an academic goal? It is estimated that a single year's class of school dropouts will cost the nation some $240 billion in lost earnings, taxes, and added social programs over the lifetime of the dropouts. Isn't a job guarantee provided through incentives to achieve, superior to having to pay continually for those who would not pursue an education that makes them marketable? What is the difference between the cost of a job guarantee and having to provide total or intermittent welfare, unemployment, or imprisonment? What is wrong with rescinding the driver's license of dropouts as an incentive to encourage them to complete school to achieve a marketable education? What is wrong with having a minimum living wage for high school graduates and a lower minimum wage for dropouts? However, such incentives must be combined with a full employment policy, so the negative impact won't befall minorities and the disadvantaged disproportionately, as happens in a flawed unfettered capitalist economic system.

As another incentive, students must be provided every opportunity to be introduced to the vast number of careers that are available in the world. Far too many students graduate from high school or drop out without having been introduced to career opportunities other than those of their parents, friends, relatives, or the local fast food outlet. Greater emphasis at an early age must be placed on the introduction of students to careers, all careers. Ambition and purpose can be powerful motivators for students in their need to know why an education is so important. If the introduction of career choices will result in more students completing school rather than dropping out, the effort will be more than worth it to society. Career introduction could be a part of the partnership that must develop between all three sectors of the Social Capitalist economic system. Businesses should be encouraged through incentives to provide apprenticeship and training programs that will lead to full-time gainful employment, possibly in partnership with educational facilities.

8.2   Teacher Involvement

A key component in improving an educational system is to get teachers involved in the administration of schools. School system employees, and especially highly educated teachers, have the intelligence to contribute and must be allowed to do so. It is ludicrous to require that teachers be highly educated to fulfill the requirements of their positions, then for school systems not to tap that knowledge in the administration of education. As in the economy, schools are in the business of teaching, where there must be a partnership between management and employees, or administration and teachers. As in the private sector, until the brains of teachers are utilized fully in the business of education, maximum efficiency in education will never be achieved.

Teachers, who have the closest contact with students and are most likely to recognize their education needs, must be partners in the administration of schools and not be subordinated and treated as adversaries by administrators and school boards.

One tool that should be taught to every student is to think and, by thinking, to be able to reason logically. One who thinks and reasons logically cannot be led unless he or she wishes to be led. Everyone can think, but the art of reasonable, logical thinking or critical thinking can lead to a very rewarding life. When students do not learn to think critically and logically, their opportunity to lead rather than follow is diminished. Life is a constant road of choices. To be able to make the logical, reasonable choices can provide the edge that may lead to prosperity over life's challenges. America must provide for the proper education of students in this dynamic society and economic system. Education must incorporate the ability to think and reason logically into the education of students as an attribute that greatly enhances employability in any dynamic economic environment. For he or she who would act and lead from logical reasoning is a true leader and much more employable in a Social Capitalist economic system.

8.3   Business Education and Involvement

Looking at the success of new businesses, or in many cases the lack thereof, it is disheartening to find that in the first year of operation an estimated 40 percent of new businesses fail. In the first seven years of operation, an estimated 90 percent of new businesses fail. Many would find this amazing, given that an estimated 80 percent of citizens would like to own and operate their own business. Logically, however, it should not be amazing to learn of such high failure rates. In fact, it should be amazing to find any other statistics than these, given the lack of required business, technical, or economics training in the education systems.

America is a dynamic society. It has moved from an agricultural-based economy to an industrial-based economy and now to a technology and services-based economy. With an industrial and technology-based economy comes business. Most American adults conduct business every day of their lives. Yet, most Americans can complete twelve years of public education and even four years of higher education and not be required to take a single business or economics class. Why, then, shouldn't there be a high number of failures in new businesses, when there is no required training through the education system? At the same time, the complexity of starting and operating a business increases annually. It is no longer adequate to teach just literacy; there must also be teaching in more advanced fields to keep up with a dynamic environment.

Under Social Capitalism the nationwide computer-based employment network must be enhanced in which the private and public sectors would list employment openings, and the unemployed, underemployed, and graduating students would list their qualifications to find matches for gainful employment.

The complexity of starting or running a business today is far greater than in the past. There has not been a significant change in the educational systems in this country to address these greater complexities, or business education at all, for that matter. Under a system of Social Capitalism, the private sector employers must align with education to support mutually beneficial efforts. Public educational systems need to know what the private sector needs in the way of skills of employees. The private sector needs employees with marketable skills, especially in the areas of business, economics, technology, and logical reasoning. Social Capitalist economic policy must ensure that the private sector and the public educational systems are aligned toward common goals. This alignment can even be to the point of the recruitment of students by industries as an incentive for recruited students to excel in a particular field.

8.4   Higher Education Financing

Every student must have equal access to education. Not all students are qualified for college, but every student should be provided the opportunity for higher education, be it college, trade schools, vocational schools, business schools, etc. Every free public educational facility or combination of facilities must have the capacity to offer the full range of opportunity that is available at other facilities. Education is not a commodity. Communities should not have to compete for students. Competition for students will lead to the wealthy in wealthy communities becoming wealthier and the poor in poorer communities falling by the wayside. This need not be. Standardized education, with standardized government support as the right of all students, can keep education and opportunity alive for all students under Social Capitalism, regardless of their social standing. Social Capitalism would provide free public education not only through high school, but through higher education as well. The emphasis must be on excellence in education, not profits for capitalists. Under the current unfettered capitalist economic system and the push by capitalists for charter school education, the emphasis is on profits at the expense of a decent public education at public expense. The privatization of campus dorms is another way that capitalists extract student loan funds from students and leave the students with monster debt, diminished employment opportunities due to the exportation of jobs, and laws that prevent student loans from being forgiven through bankruptcy.

All graduating high school students must be afforded a publicly funded higher education or training without regard to the social or economic status of parents.

A Social Capitalist economic system must provide free public education so that the playing field is leveled for all students. If education is based on ability to pay or ability to get grants or loans that have to be repaid, the students of the working class are at a substantial disadvantage in the employment arena. Such practices perpetuate the rich getting richer and the poor getting poorer. To deprive a student of the opportunity for a higher education because the parents are supposedly of such a financial capacity as to disqualify the student for loans or grants is not a level playing field and must be replaced under Social Capitalism with free public postsecondary education.

"Freedom from fear is eternally linked with freedom
from want."
—Franklin D. Roosevelt

9.   Social Security

In a civilized society and a capitalist economic system, it is entirely logical that the working class have retirement funds available to them when their working days are over. Retirement funds would be set aside by the working class during their productive years if wages and salaries provided a living. In a trickle-down economy, where the majority of income goes to the wealthy, as in greedy capitalists, too many of the working class are unable to set aside funds in retirement plans. This was recognized by Franklin D. Roosevelt in the Social Security Act of 1935. The failure of capitalists to provide adequately for the working class rightfully brought about a government program to provide old age benefits to the retired working class.

Capitalists that accumulate obscene wealth do not have to worry about having an adequate retirement income. In addition and in keeping with their quest for profits and wealth at all costs, the cost of retirement programs for the retired working class is not acceptable to these capitalists under an unfettered capitalism economic system, and they would prefer to see the Social Security program, as with the Medicare program, eliminated.

"I never think of the future. It comes soon enough."
—Albert Einstein

The American Social Security program and the Medicare program have been heralded by many not only to be great social programs, but programs that should be expanded. Once again, whether the two programs are heralded or denounced generally depends on whether an individual is a capitalist or of the working class. The original Social Security Act and amendments intended that there be a Social Security Trust Fund. All monies paid into the Social Security program would be placed in the trust fund, and all Social Security payments would be paid out of the fund. At the present time there is still a trust fund on paper, but there isn't any money in the trust fund, just IOUs, so to speak. However, there still exists an obligation through the Social Security Act for the government to make all required Social Security payments. It is the collection of taxes that is so objectionable to the capitalists. Therefore, the capitalists want to eliminate the Social Security and Medicare programs. If the programs are eliminated, they believe that no taxes would have to be collected to cover the costs of the two programs, and they could continue to receive tax cuts to stockpile obscene wealth. Capitalists continually argue that it is entitlements like Social Security, Medicare, and Medicaid that have caused the enormous national debt and the entitlements must be changed, reduced, privatized, or eliminated to get the country out of the debt it is in. The argument is false. The argument is a blatant attempt by the greedy capitalists to scare politicians into making changes to the entitlements to divert attention from the real debt creators, which are tax cuts for the wealthy, wars, excessive defense spending, corporate subsidies, and other wasteful spending. The true fix to the entitlements is to rescind the tax cuts for the wealthy and adopt a Social Capitalist economic system. Under Social Capitalism, Social Security, Medicare, and Medicaid would not only be continued but be expanded in keeping with the provision of a living wage and benefits.

The confusion over the Social Security Trust Fund began when Congress began borrowing from the trust fund for other government expenditures. In place of the borrowed funds, Congress gave IOUs to the fund with the intent of paying the money back at some point in the future. The point of repayment came during the Reagan administration, but, true to form, the funds to repay the trust fund were given away under false pretenses to the capitalists in the form of tax cuts to the wealthy. When the funds were available to pay back to the Social Security trust fund, a capitalist administration paid it out in tax cuts for the wealthy that paid little or nothing into Social Security in the first place. This charade is taking the working class for a ride by pilfering the trust funds for distribution to the wealthy. The false pretenses worked so well that future presidents began giving the capitalists even more tax cuts. Even with the unprecedented tax cuts to the wealthy, they still aren't satisfied and will not be satisfied until their tax rate is zero and the working class shoulders the entire tax funding burden for the government, which pushes more and more citizens into poverty.

Under a Social Capitalist economic system, the government taxes collected from the wealthy by controlling greed and removing the cap on all payrolls for Social Security taxes would be more than enough to fund the Social Security and Medicare programs for perpetuity, even with expansion of both programs. The necessity for Social Security and Medicare is the result of a failure by capitalists to pay living wages and benefits to the working class. Therefore, with both programs being retained and expanded under Social Capitalism, it should be the capitalists that pay the majority of the taxes to support the working class. This will be accomplished by elimination of the cap on income subject to the Social Security and Medicare taxes.

Even under Social Capitalism, a program to provide retirement income to the unemployable will be needed. The working class would be able to set aside funds in individual retirement accounts (IRAs), thus reducing the reliance on government programs. In addition, if national single-payer health care is provided as a benefit to the working class, Medicare could be retained similar to what it is to cover retirees. Also, by gaining the highest degree of education or training, individuals could receive additional benefits like bonuses or other incentives to enhance their retirement. This could lead to enhanced productivity and cooperation in the workplace as businesses offer bonuses to IRAs for excellence in production. Any number of additional benefits and achievements could be realized through such programs. This is yet another case for the elimination of unfettered capitalism in favor of Social Capitalism.

Company pension funds are similar to Social Security and IRAs in providing retirement funds for the working class. Company pension funds are usually negotiated periodically as part of wages and salaries. However, federal laws allow a company that falls on hard times to use the pension funds in order to remain solvent. This is akin to stealing the pension funds from employees, especially when the hard times are contrived in order to attach the pension funds. Once again, greed finds its way into the picture. Under Social Capitalism any negotiated pension funds must be as a contribution to the IRAs of employees such that the funds cannot be used by the company under any circumstances. Under Social Capitalism, it must become unlawful for capitalists to shut down a company simply to enhance profits by the shutdown. Before a company could be shut down simply to profiteer, it must be offered to the employees or another company in order to retain the employees' jobs. Profiting greedily by the closure of a company or by moving the company to a foreign country to achieve cheaper labor and greater profits must be unlawful under a Social Capitalism economic system.

"We abuse land because we regard it as a commodity belonging to us. When we see land as a community to which we belong, we may begin to use it with love and respect."

—Aldo Leopold

10. Environment

There is no longer any question that an unfettered capitalist economy, left unchecked, can have a devastating impact on the environment. Government must become the public's check on capitalism by the adoption of Social Capitalism to ensure that the environmental interests of the public are upheld. The natural resources of a nation cannot be ravaged for a profit-motivated unfettered capitalist system without adequate protection of the public and the environment. Global climate change can no longer be denied by greedy capitalists in order for them to continue to pollute and ravage the environment into utter devastation in the name of corporate profits. There must be an acceptable medium between the use of resources, provision of jobs, and protection of the environment when utilizing natural resources.

Natural resources must be utilized to the degree necessary and also protected to the degree that it will not interfere with the survival of a democracy. Natural resources must be utilized by mankind in a responsible manner, not just to enhance capitalist profits. Natural resources cannot be abused under the premise of profits at all costs, but rather must be utilized to provide jobs in consideration of the cost. The cost consideration is multifaceted. It is not just the cutting of a tree or the removal of ore from an open pit mine that must be done responsibly. It is also the cost to the environment and future generations after the tree is cut and the ore is mined that must be addressed environmentally.

Natural resources belong not only to everyone in a democratic nation but to future generations, and private sector developers must compensate the taxpayers accordingly.

The land in a democratic nation belongs to all the people. There is temporary title to the land as held by individuals, corporations, businesses, etc., for use, but what happens when the individuals, corporations, or businesses are gone? Who does the land revert to then? The land will revert to the government, which is the people, the future generations. Every citizen is a steward of all the land in a democratic nation. Every pile of garbage that is buried, every piece of trash that is thrown from a vehicle, is disposed of onto all the people's land. If every individual, corporation, business, and government treated all the land as if it were their own, which it theoretically is, it would be a better place for all. Unfortunately, there are those who would abuse the land as if it were theirs and theirs alone to profit from as they please.

To protect the land, the natural resources, and the environment from those who would abuse them, there must be laws to uphold the land belonging to everyone in a democratic nation. What is wrong with requiring those who would profit from the taking of natural resources to restore the land to the greatest possible benefit of future generations? If trees are cut, why is it not required that trees are to be replaced one for one as part of the logging process? If ore is mined, the land or property must be restored as nearly as possible to the original condition. As rivers are dammed and oil is pumped, it must be done with the least potential harm to the environment.

Under unfettered capitalism, so-called scarce natural resources that belong to the public are often made

available to private sector enterprises with minimal or
no meaningful return to the taxpayers.

Equal economic opportunity must mean that equal benefit is derived from natural resources, and equal attention is provided to ensure that the least amount of damage is left behind for future generations. No longer can it be allowed that capitalists will profit while the working class gets nothing and the government cleans up the mess. No longer can it be left solely up to big business to determine what is best for a democracy. The American economic system, once it evolves into a three-party partnership, would involve each of the three parties in determining what is best for the natural resources. As technology advances, the reliance on natural resources may diminish, but the protection of what does remain must be shared by all parties. The result of the taking of natural resources must be reclamation of the area for future generations, not devastation left because of a profit motive.

Environmental policy must include provision for the care, use, preservation, restoration, and replenishment of natural resources. Lakes and streams cannot be allowed to be devastated as a ramification of the clear cutting of timber. Clear cutting of timber is not necessary; it is just profitable. There are other ways that must be used, like strip cutting with replanting. Once the replant is established, the next strip can be cut and so on. The government and industry must think of what is best for all, not for the profits of a select few capitalists. Leadership with integrity, statesmanship/stateswomanship, and sound business sense in the interest of the people will see that the natural resources are properly utilized and protected for everyone under a Social Capitalist economic system.

As previously stated, the fuel that drives an economy is jobs. The fuel that drives jobs is energy, as was so emphatically pointed out during the supposed energy crisis of the seventies. As the cost of energy goes, so goes a huge portion of an economy, including jobs. Common knowledge indicates that the energy from some fossil fuels will be depleted at some point in the future. It is logical to conclude a significant effort should be placed on the need for developing renewable energy sources for use before supplies of fossil fuels are depleted. Alternative energy would already be a reality if the economic system were Social Capitalism. It is not a reality because of unfettered capitalism and the profits at all costs of capitalists.

Under Social Capitalism there must be a decisive plan to effectively and adequately support the development and production of significant renewable energy resources. It is almost as if the government is riding on the hope that something will miraculously appear one day that will resolve all future energy problems and needs. That's like going to war without ammunition on the bet that the enemy won't fire. America needs an energy policy that will promote renewable energy resource development, promote jobs, and ensure that future energy needs are indeed going to be met. Goals, objectives, logic, and reason will provide for future energy needs, not imports, hope, and leadership driven by special interest oil company profits.

There is no question that there must be consideration for the environment in deciding on development, land use, solid waste, resources, and pollutants. There must be a plan that is logically derived and considerate of all aspects of life. Every human being is a shepherd of this planet, and no one should proceed with the pursuit of wealth at enormous costs to the environment. Money should not be the primary pursuit of mankind. The productive use of resources must include the recycling of the by-products. Protection of the environment must be of equal or greater emphasis than wealth. Job creation and the accumulation of wealth are two different emphases. We must utilize resources and recycled resources to create jobs in harmony with the environment, not at the expense of the environment for the accumulation of wealth and the ultimate destruction of the planet.

Capitalists, voters, and consumers must recognize that the economic production, distribution, and consumption process is not complete until pollution, waste, and potential environmental damage are reclaimed or recycled under a Social Capitalist economic system, and must exercise their votes accordingly.

A most effective program that will begin to address environmental issues, short of shutting down all industry, is recycling. Recycling must become mandatory. Industry must be held accountable for their products and what they produce, to the point that they become responsible for the recycling or safe disposal of what they produce. Industry must gear up for recycling even to the point of deposits on all containers produced and marketed by industry. New industries must be pursued and developed that will make the greatest use of recycled materials many times over. If necessary, government incentives must be introduced to encourage the development, use, and reuse of recycled materials. With responsible leadership will come responsible policies based on Social Capitalism. Industry can no longer be allowed to continue to bury, burn, or sink garbage into the next generations under the pretense of an unfettered capitalist economy. A free market economy does not mean free to do as the capitalist pleases in the quest of profits. It means free to pursue a venture or career in a socially and environmentally responsible manner.

A capitalist system does not necessarily provide for recycling or replenishing; it basically provides that the means of production and distribution are privately owned. There is no inherent drive for industry to replenish resources or reclaim and recycle products. The drive is for profits and wealth. The check on this drive in the interest and protection of the working class must be the inclusion of government in a Social Capitalist economic system. Government will continue to be the one who will be stuck with the cleanup bills from the abuses of the profit-motivated unfettered capitalist economic system. A three-party partnership in the economy would provide the proper stewardship needed to ensure that recycling is a part of the economic system. Companies, corporations, and stockholders can no longer be allowed to reap the profits of capitalist production and leave the working class to pay for cleaning up the residue. Government legislation must hold producers accountable for what they produce, by way of a Social Capitalist economic system.

The government must implement provisions that require accountability, especially in recycling. The working class must become fully aware of what products are recyclable and what companies are environmentally conscious, and exercise their support accordingly. By such measures those companies that are less than environmentally sound will justly fall by the wayside. In their place, new environmentally sound companies will emerge and the nation will benefit. It is just as wrong for consumers to support irresponsible actions by manufacturers whose products are environmentally inconsiderate. Consumers and voters must support environmentally sound businesses and industries and avoid the rest if at all possible.

With government policies like employment incentives, guaranteed loans, and investment credits that promote businesses in the interest of jobs, the minds in America will go to work. The brain power that is in America will find ways to deal with recycled resources that haven't even been imagined yet. Products and services will emerge to utilize and reclaim millions of tons of what is now considered waste, not only once, but for reuse two, three, and four times or more. To the same end, as regulations are enacted to prohibit the disposal of certain materials, additional industries will be generated to provide alternative environmentally sound products and services. The key to this entire effort is to turn the power of the entrepreneur loose on the issue through incentives that promote and encourage such development. In addition, the government must review existing policies that may be disincentives to recycle or reclaim. If disincentives are found, legislation must be enacted that will provide incentives to recycle and reclaim that would be in addition to the pressure from consumers. Any government policies, whether federal, state, or local, to encourage recycling must provide for consumers to be able to recycle everything conveniently. Consumers, as the taxpayers who will be stuck with paying for the cost of environmental damage in the future, must recycle as much waste as possible to minimize the burden on future generations. The people must see that action is taken at the polls to elect those who will protect the nation, not those who succumb to the powers of wealth, greed, and selfishness.

A democracy must enact a logical plan with both short-term and long-term components that will set in motion a nonpolluting nation. It must also provide for the enjoyment of life by everyone, free from pollutants or the threat of pollutants. Penalties for polluting must be severe enough to deter any and all pollution. We need only look at the climate change that is occurring to know that something is going on. We cannot wait until the day we learn irreparable damage has been done to the planet as a result of pollution. Future generations deserve better.

Government policies, incentives, and penalties must be geared toward the elimination of pollutants. It is not acceptable to have policies which provide that if a company or individual can afford the penalty or fee, he, she, or it may go ahead and pollute. Automobile makers, for instance, must be required to provide a standard level of nonpollution for *all* vehicles. Government must set a plan in motion that will not succumb to the powers of wealth and greed and that will in fact result in clean air for all. Policies that respect health, inspire nonpolluting development, provide equality, address global warming, and preserve the ozone layer are right for every nation. The contention by capitalists that global warming or climate change is not occurring, so therefore they may continue to ravage the environment for greed and profits, can no longer be tolerated. The environment and responsibility for care of the environment belongs to everyone. The disposition of the environment cannot be left to the capitalists for more profits at the expense of the working class. Once consumed with greed, the greedy have no boundaries over obscene profits and wealth accumulation, even when it comes to the environment and preservation of human life.

Government policy must be toward the goal of a nonpolluting nation, where groundwater contamination cannot be allowed at any cost. Consumers must insist that local governments begin looking into mass transit, recycling, and reclamation requirements at all levels of society. As a nation, we must even look to the point of stockpiling recyclables for which there are uses yet to be developed.

All the concerns addressed toward protection of clean air must also be addressed to the protection of groundwater, lakes, rivers, and oceans. To this end, "an ounce of prevention is worth a pound of cure" is no more true anywhere than in dealing with water. Significant efforts must be made to protect groundwater from chemicals, disposal sites, spills, and any other contaminants that will leach into the aquifers, drinking water, lakes, rivers, and oceans.

"Only a socially just country has the right to exist."
—Pope John Paul II

11. Justice

As with the rest of the problems in a democracy, the solution to a legal system in chaos is multifaceted. A flawed capitalist economic system causes ethnic minorities and the less fortunate to be subordinated to nonminorities in their search for employment. The unfettered capitalist economic system, including employment, is dominated by nonminorities. Therefore, it would follow logically that a greater frustration with the system would be concentrated with the less fortunate and in minority communities. Such a disparity can lead to a perceived double standard in the legal system which processes them in a disproportionate number. This perceived double standard becomes very real for those who end up on the wrong end of the system for lack of employment opportunities.

Since the economic system does not provide equal economic or employment opportunity, it impoverishes minorities and the less fortunate, who may then be more tempted to resort to criminal activities not only to survive but also as a protest of the flawed economic system, resulting in a greater number being involved in legal problems or incarceration.

Capitalists and the employed have a means of providing for their families. Such individuals are less likely to revert to criminal activities in their drive for survival that could lead to involvement at the wrong end of the law. In an unfettered capitalist economic system, the rich will get richer as long as there are no changes that would improve participation by minorities and the less fortunate. Without change to Social Capitalism, there will always be the possibility that the frustrated will revert to survival instincts, which may include criminal activity. If an individual has nothing to lose, the "correctional" system is less intimidating and therefore less of a deterrent to criminal activities. As long as a disproportionate number of minorities are incarcerated by the legal system, one could think that the capitalist-controlled legal system is designed to keep minorities in check for the capitalists. Of course, this may not be true, but perception can be as bad as reality in some cases. Equal economic opportunity under Social Capitalism is the alternative to the incarceration of frustrated minorities and the less fortunate.

Many people who are incarcerated are there because of a flawed economic system and must be given a second chance if they are not violent or habitual offenders, through true rehabilitation, not confined to a privatized prison that doesn't correct anything. Public rehabilitation facilities that will develop the various skills of those incarcerated, so they can be productively returned to society and a Social Capitalist economic system must be developed.

Government economic policy must include equal opportunity for all Americans, free from racism, discrimination, and bigotry. All people have the right to be accepted for who they are, not what they are. Government and society must recognize and support this concept through all actions undertaken that affect life in a democracy. No individual deserves to be discriminated against because of his or her race, color, religion, or walk of life. This does not mean, however, that individuals who purposefully physically harm others cannot earn the right to be treated other than as decent people. Criminals who are violent, habitual offenders earn the right to be treated as less than decent citizens and do not deserve a second chance. The actions and remarks of these individuals, regardless of race, color, religion, or walk of life, earn them the right to be treated differently. However, this individual difference should have no reflection on their entire race, color, religion, or walk of life as a whole. Social Capitalism can significantly turn the nation in a new direction and away from discrimination.

Since no child ever born unto this earth had a choice as to his or her birthright, then racism, discrimination, and bigotry have no place in any society.

A legal system that breeds disgust and contempt from those who serve it is wrong. The actions by police personnel to bring criminals and violent offenders to justice should not be negated by the courts and the legal system. What good is a system where police leave a courtroom shaking their heads because a violent or habitual offender was released again? How does this action protect law-abiding citizens? The system must be respected, but respect is earned, not commanded. This is what can happen when the economic system does not serve all the people. Respect for the legal system is earned by doing the job that was intended. A revolving door does not serve anyone except the violent habitual offenders that are going through it. Violent or habitual criminals are criminals and they must be locked up as the system intended. Nonhabitual, nonviolent offenders must be rehabilitated as the system intended.

In the commission of illegal acts other than cases involving violence, causing the injury, abuse, or death of an individual once may be a mistake, but twice is a habit, and illegal habits by violent habitual offenders must be punished.

The first step in cleaning up a criminal justice system is to establish full employment at a living wage and benefits and equal economic opportunity under Social Capitalism. Full employment does not mean almost full employment with a waiting list, as in a percentage of the working class on unemployment. Until equality of opportunity is afforded everyone, anything done to improve the criminal justice system is an effort in futility. As long as the less fortunate and minorities are shut out of the economic picture, there will be a reversion to criminal activity as a perceived means of gaining equality. It won't matter if the perpetrators are incarcerated or not; without gainful employment opportunities there will continue to be a reversion to the perceived equalizer, which is criminal activity. Therefore, implementation of equal economic opportunity under a Social Capitalist economic system is a first step in correcting a criminal justice system.

A contributing factor to the number of minorities and others that end up in the legal system, and for that matter for most that end up in legal trouble, is unemployment or employment at less than a living wage. This is not the result of being a minority or disadvantaged; it is designed into the system. The majority-dominated capitalist economic system discriminates against those who make up the minorities and less fortunate of the working class. With such a system, and human nature being more comfortable with their own, minorities will continue to suffer. No amount of regulation or control can change instinctive habits, but a change to an equal opportunity Social Capitalist economic system can.

Discrimination and racism are not a result of only skin color, religion, etc., but rather of the poverty into which an unjust society has locked people. Racism is a convenient outlet for the animosity that builds within the employed toward those perceived as living off the taxpayers as users of the system. The greatest contributor to racism is poverty that is perpetrated on minorities and the less fortunate because of the greed of capitalists and lack of an equitable economic policy of full employment at a living wage and benefits. It is amazing how the employed are accepted and the unemployed are discriminated against. It would be interesting to see what would happen if every able-bodied person was employed at a living wage under Social Capitalism.

Without full employment opportunity for all, those who would act in the interest of their own survival cannot be condemned. A true democracy does not shut out its ethnic minority populations from the workforce and then blame them for acting in their own best interests to survive. If the elite who have a conscience but do not believe in a policy of full employment would walk in the shoes of the unemployed and face the same conditions of hopelessness, they would quickly provide for full employment at a living wage.

Discrimination and racism are perpetuated where the majority of businesses are owned by the majority race. Left unchecked, the majority race will employ members of the same race, which means nonemployment of minorities. Again, it is the stigma attached to minorities by the associated poverty caused by the lack of equal economic opportunity from an undeclared unfettered capitalist economic policy that causes unequal employment opportunity. Change the economic policy and discrimination diminishes proportionately. Government must provide the checks and regulations that will create the opportunity of employment for all, including minorities.

The cause of civil disturbances in areas of high concentrations of ethnic unemployment is abuse and mistreatment by a flawed economic system, which must be corrected with Social Capitalism.

There are those of some influence that do not believe that minorities and the disadvantaged have a right to feel as though they have been left out of the economy. These influential people state that if such minorities and disadvantaged would quit complaining and feeling sorry for themselves and get out and get a job, they would be a part of the economy. Such statements are shallow responses to complex problems brought on by flawed capitalist theory, and for which the expounders have no other answers.

Flawed government economic policy creates victims every bit as blatantly as the resulting crimes committed by individuals.

Incarceration institutions must be public to deal with nonviolent criminals and violent or habitual offenders, and must be identified as serving one of two purposes. Either an institution is a punishment facility for violent criminals or habitual offenders who would harm or kill others, or a rehabilitation facility in which nonviolent criminals will be rehabilitated and returned to society. The key here is punishment for hardened criminals and rehabilitation for the nonviolent. Those who are hardened criminals or felons would be committed to an institution as an end in itself, unless the crime merited rehabilitation after the term of punishment. Nonviolent offenders would be rehabilitated through a system of facilities set up nationally, whereby each facility would specialize in a particular craft, trade, or profession.

Inmates, according to skills, preferences, testing, and screening, would be provided opportunities to participate in the rehabilitation facility most likely to result in the end product of a productive citizen. For instance, one facility may be set up to rehabilitate by affording inmates the completion of a higher education. Another facility may be set up as a trade school in which those selected could further develop trades or interests as their rehabilitation. Another facility may train drivers or equipment operators, while another may be a high-technology facility to train computer operators, programmers, technicians, and so on. In any event, under a Social Capitalist economic system, the institutions of confinement or rehabilitation will be operated by the government and not privatized to afford more taxpayer profits to the greedy capitalists.

Provide for a government-set procedure nationally that will standardize the guidelines that will determine punishment or rehabilitation of those convicted through the legal system.

It must be realized that there is a little good in everyone and that circumstances can sometimes result in actions unbecoming a particular individual. Such individuals must be given a second chance, and incarceration without rehabilitation serves absolutely no one. The cost is exorbitant, the inmates generate hatred for the democracy and economic system that failed them, and their incarceration is spent devising plans for how to get even. Many people are inmates because of the failure of the unfettered capitalist system to account for them. To compound the failure of the system, when they do make a mistake and develop a bad habit, it fails them again by locking them up and forgetting about them until they are to be released. There is a better way, and that is a second chance through true rehabilitation. The taxpayers, who must foot the bill for incarceration, deserve a better return on their investment. The better deal is to spend the money to produce a productive citizen, not a repeat offender. However, the first step must be provision for equal economic opportunity and full employment so the rehabilitated can be gainfully employed after their incarceration. In any case, the penal institutions must be public and not private. The quest for profits by capitalists that operate private institutions could lead to a charade of rehabilitation rather than real rehabilitation so the cells can be occupied longer for more profits off the taxpayers.

*"The generality of men are naturally apt to be swayed
by fear rather than reverence, and to refrain from evil
rather because of the punishment that it brings than
because of its own foulness."*
—Aristotle

Revision of the legal incarceration system is not a stand-alone act.
There must be changes to eradicate racism, joblessness, homelessness,
drugs, and abuse of others. All efforts must go hand in hand. It must
be recognized there are some people who cannot get along in society
no matter what is done to prevent their actions. Such individuals must
be removed from society for the protection of others and for their own
protection. It must also be recognized that having a justice system that
places killers in prison with shoplifters cannot benefit either party. This
outcome is already identified by the number of repeat offenders that
return to prison. Therefore, the justice system must be revised to identify
and provide that every facility designed for incarceration is specified
for one of the two purposes. They must either be designated as a penal
institution for the punishment of violent criminals, or designated a
rehabilitation facility for nonviolent offenders. If necessary, additional
facilities must be constructed to accommodate this separation.

Education, as previously stated, must extend into the legal system
through the rehabilitation of nonviolent offenders. The forces in an
unequal economic society that result in acts that lead to incarceration,
especially of minorities, must become a means to a second opportunity
for society to provide a productive individual. Every human being
has a brain. It must be the responsibility of a just society to see that
all brains are developed for productive purposes. If society fails once,
it cannot and must not give up, but rather, if the opportunity arises,
try again. Such is the opportunity in the legal system, but only if
it is recognized and designed to do so in conjunction with a Social
Capitalist economic system.

Unemployment, which can include poverty or a lack of hope, can lead to involvement in illegal drugs. The mandate of society which requires that every adult citizen must have a source of income to survive can be a powerful motivator to seek money of any kind. That motivation should be toward getting a job and thereby a source of income, if there are jobs. However, when there is a lack of jobs and therefore a lack of hope, the motivation can be toward an effort to get money from whatever source and at whatever risk. Such an attitude can lead to the perceived "get rich quick" world of selling illegal drugs, or using illegal drugs to escape reality.

To combat continued rationalization for becoming involved in the illegal drug trade, there must be an opportunity of employment for everyone. With employment comes a sense of belonging, of participating, of being accepted. Self-esteem rises and the necessities of life become possible. Under a Social Capitalist economic system, government must use every means at its disposal to provide the incentives for establishing jobs in business and industry as alternatives to drug dealing. In addition, once a full employment policy that provides opportunity and hope has been adopted, the penalty for dealing drugs must be made so severe that the alternative, employment, will be chosen.

Alternatives must be provided to the children to concentrate their efforts, ambitions, and energy in productive rather than destructive ways. Whatever the cost may be to provide alternatives, those costs will never be greater than the loss of a single child to the world of illegal drugs. Alternatives can be in the form of teen centers, community service activities, and involving children in government, business, sports, and community events. Children have an unlimited energy that, if not provided an opportunity to develop in a productive manner, can just as easily develop in a less-than-productive manner. With the demise of the traditional family, society must contribute every effort toward providing alternatives before it is too late, since the cost to society after it is too late is much greater.

Neither the legal system nor the US Constitution guarantees that the guilty will be punished or that the innocent will go free. It is guaranteed that in most cases the accused will be given fair treatment. The accused, found to be guilty as a result of such fair treatment, are not assuredly criminals; they have only been found guilty. Unless those found guilty of crimes are assured to be guilty of the crime through such things as DNA testing, there should be no death penalty, but rather life in prison without parole. If additional evidence is put forth in the future, every opportunity to prove the individual not guilty should be provided by the legal system.

Capital punishment has both strong proponents and strong opponents, for very good reasons. It is logical that an individual be put to death if guilty of taking another's life, but only if guilt is assured through forensics such as DNA testing.

Capital punishment must be standardized nationwide to ensure its use in appropriate cases, and to ensure it is not abused on technicalities. In capital punishment cases there is no logic, either morally or legally, that should preclude the reexamination of a case based on future developments or evidence.

As has been stated time and time again in all walks of life, the children are the future. Yet, when the unfettered capitalism economic system is evaluated, there must be concern for the neglect of the children. Not all children, for sure, but enough of the children so there is reason to be concerned. In years gone by, children were needed on the farms to help with the field work. Children, even in the urban areas, had chores to do that kept them busy and occupied. This is no longer the case. Hand labor and chores have given way to machines and appliances. This has left the children with idle time that has not been filled with productive actions in all too many cases. Television has become a standard that fills roles from teacher to baby sitter to idea generator. Not all that comes out of the television is productive! This is probably not what is desired as the future for children! The needs of the children in a changing nation must be met by provision for channeling their energy into productive undertakings. If left unchallenged, the energy of children can be put to use in illegal activities.

Children have been left out of the race for a better life, except as the recipients of "having it better than I did." Children are intelligent, productive human beings if allowed to be so. They should be acknowledged as such and treated accordingly under a Social Capitalist economic system. A democratic nation must do the best job it can do when it comes to providing avenues for the children to explore, learn, contribute, participate, and grow into the leaders of tomorrow.

Children are products of their environment, not of their heritage. The ideal situation for any child is to be brought into this world to a loving, understanding family that expounds love for all mankind. Unfortunately, this ideal situation does not happen for all children. It is probably safe to say that it does not happen in a majority of cases. In those cases where it does happen, it is good, and the children are lucky. In those cases where it does not happen, society must take the necessary steps to ensure that these children have every opportunity to lead normal productive lives. All children have heroes—their parents—until or unless their image is shattered by unemployment, abuse, or other unfortunate circumstances, and many children will generally emulate their parents, whether good, bad, or indifferent.

To provide the avenue for children, youngsters through teenagers, to learn and grow in a responsible environment, it is proposed that communities, in a Social Capitalist economic system, develop public teen centers. Teen centers would be an alternative to being home alone, in gangs, or on the streets for lack of any available activities. These teen centers are not just the refurbishing of old unwanted buildings into a place for kids to hang out. They would be strategically designed complexes that would provide a learning, fun environment for children to develop and grow during nonschool hours. They would be complete with supervision, guidance, assistance, tutors, counseling, and rules, and without the hypocrisy, racism, and bigotry that affect their lives before they have had a real chance to develop.

Children must be afforded the opportunity to interact with elders, possibly as a school activity or in day care centers for both children and elders, to learn values that have been developed from experience.

The teen centers would be a link to the community and to community events sponsored by the centers. They would provide for activities in a wide range of areas and interests that would expose the real world to the children. The whole concept of teen centers is to put money into the development of children, rather than into their rehabilitation when it may be too late for many. Most kids have a strong desire to contribute, learn, and show what they can do. The problem is that few if any avenues exist which will provide this opportunity. Teen centers must be developed that would be an investment in the children to develop as productive adults, not in need of reform or rehabilitation.

A center is envisioned that would be large enough to support the majority of children in the community. Membership in the center would be automatic for every child, by issuance of an ID card that will allow the child to gain entry. Membership could be suspended or reverted to a probationary period by the center's board of directors at any time that the individual broke the rules or otherwise became a distraction in the center. Full membership would only be reinstated upon the suspended or probationary individual meeting certain requirements. There would be constant supervision, both paid and volunteered. There would be video monitors throughout the center to assure that rules are being observed and that all members are secure and safe. There would be such a wide range of activities available that virtually every individual member would find something that interests him or her, or would be able to explore new activities that would otherwise be unavailable. There would be sports areas for basketball, hockey, batting practice, roller and ice skating, exercise training, body building, pool, bowling, and any number of other sports. There would be a game area for videos, chess, and quiz games where tournaments could be set up if of interest to the members. There would be washroom facilities and locker rooms to support the activities. Eventually, teen centers could become community centers for all to utilize and enjoy. Teen centers in communities would be provided as a supervised alternative for children from gangs, the streets, fractured homes, and the lack of parental guidance.

There could be a library or reading area where members could get help from other members or tutors in developing their academics. Members could bring their parents or grandparents or others to the center. Elders in the community could volunteer their abilities to the center to help members in any way that the imagination can provide. Industry, business, and civic leaders could put on seminars and assemblies that would demonstrate or introduce members to products, vocations, opportunities, training, careers, skills, or any number of other events that would help in broadening the minds and futures of the members. The centers could sponsor training in such areas as CPR, first aid, fire prevention, and self-defense. Field trips could be set up that would introduce the members to the world around them. Interest at the centers would be to promote interaction between races, intellectual groups, and ages, to show children at a young age that racism and hatred are not the norm. Children must be provided such an atmosphere in which they can develop their minds and abilities without fear of pain, suffering, ridicule, or abuse, all in keeping with democracy and a Social Capitalist economic system.

The centers would have rules and requirements that would have to be followed to retain membership in good standing. The centers would be run as nonprofit institutions so all proceeds could be channeled to the development of the members. The centers would sponsor community events on a regular basis. These events could range anywhere from an annual city cleanup day to painting the homes of elders, mowing the lawns of the disadvantaged, removing snow from hydrants, providing security services to the elderly, and anything else that would make the community a safer, better place to live for everyone. As a part of membership, each individual would be required to participate in at least one community activity annually. As members grow and graduate from school to go on to a profession, they would also graduate from their membership in the center. When they graduate, their name, picture, plaque, or other representation would be fixed in the halls of the center for posterity. The center in turn could provide a recommendation for the former member as he or she pursues his or her career.

Again, the essence of life is for every human being to do the best he or she can to make his or her life and the lives of others the best they can be. How can children even begin to move in this direction if their only contact with others is through the schools, which may have the best intentions but often have their hands full with other concerns? In addition, schools only account for a portion of a child's time. What accounts for the rest of a child's time? Children must be provided an alternative to the gangs, drugs, and warfare on the streets. Properly constructed and developed teen centers could be the alternative.

It does no good to educate and provide for the human mind to soar, and then subordinate such minds to an insignificant role in an unfettered capitalist economy. Educate the minds and then provide for all to have equal opportunity as partners in a Social Capitalist economy and the future begins to brighten.

Homelessness in a large part is the result of failed economic policy. Too many children that grow up homeless are already economically disadvantaged under unfettered capitalism. If every citizen were employed at a living wage through a full employment policy, there would be little need for subsidized housing. To dwell on the need for subsidized housing is to ignore the real issue. The concentration must be on the real issue, which is to recognize the right of equality of opportunity in the economic system. Everyone must have the opportunity to afford a home, but the money to do so must be earned by all potential home buyers, not earned by some while the government gives tax dollars to others. Failed economic policy allows the working class to provide housing to the nonworking, when many of the working class can't even afford a home themselves for lack of a living wage.

The number of families in government-subsidized housing and the number of homeless are increasing and are ample evidence of a flawed unfettered capitalist economic system.

For years the government has used the housing industry to spur the economy during slack periods. When an economic stimulus is needed, what better way than to hand out tax dollars to first-time home buyers? These are tax dollars that are collected from taxpayers during an economic downturn. How does this benefit the taxpayers who are providing the money? It doesn't, since they usually had to earn all the money to pay for their homes, while the government uses their labor to subsidize the economic recovery. Where is the equal treatment in such a system? Have the taxpayers ever been asked whether they approve of such expenditures of their taxes? The policy is a result of failed economic policy, and rather than own up to the real policy of full employment and Social Capitalism, housing subsidies are quick and easy, and who is the wiser?

Another call by an unfettered capitalist-dominated administration is to spur an economic recovery by giving tax breaks to developers. These developers are the same greedy capitalists who have already utilized a flawed capitalist economy to amass tremendous wealth under the premise of having no social responsibility. When the economy needs recovery, do these capitalists offer their wisdom and fortunes to enhance economic activity and employment? Absolutely not. Instead, they seek to exploit the devastation by crying for tax breaks and subsidies to increase their own massive holdings at the expense of the already abused working class taxpayer. To this end, there should be no such thing as tax breaks for the wealthy under the pretense of economic recovery. The direction and incentives must be to the working class for job creation and employment. Special incentives to the elite are no more than ploys to achieve funding for reelections and must be eliminated through integrity and a statesmanlike government under Social Capitalism. Working class voters must make it happen.

The entire charade of using housing to stimulate the economy would not be needed if there were a Social Capitalist economic system and a full employment policy. Such a policy would provide equal economic opportunity for everyone. A democracy needs leadership that will provide the complete solution to problems, not a temporary stimulus with taxpayer dollars every time the economy fluctuates, with the ulterior motive of reelection.

*"You will find no justification in any of the language of
the Constitution for delay in the reforms which the mass
of the American people now demand."*
—Franklin D. Roosevelt

12. Constitutional Convention

Most people recognize that the Constitution of the United States of America is the most astonishing document written by and for a free people. The foresight exercised by the framers of the US Constitution has proven to be most resilient in addressing the continuing needs of a democratic nation. Without question, the basic document should and must be retained intact as the guide for democracy. Does this mean, however, that the US Constitution is perfect and does not need to be improved from time to time? No! The framers of the US Constitution made provision for keeping the Constitution current by provision for amendments and a constitutional convention if necessary. The proof of this is also in the number of amendments that have been enacted since the passage of the US Constitution. Ten of the amendments, the Bill of Rights, were passed almost before the US Constitution was set in motion. The balance of the amendments, eleven through twenty-six, have been passed over the years in attempting to address issues of concern in a democratic nation.

The timing of a constitutional convention is absolutely critical. No constitutional convention should even be considered until a vast majority of elected positions in the federal government and the vast majority of state government elected positions are held by a democratically elected majority of the working class. If a constitutional convention were called when the capitalists held the federal government and a majority of the state governments, it would be a disaster for the working class. Most assuredly the US Constitution would be reworked to afford the unfettered capitalists a permanent hold on the government as in a plutocracy and the democracy as we know it would be lost. Since no direction is provided in the US Constitution to specify which items to change in a constitutional convention, a convention could rewrite the entire document. Of course, if the greedy were to call for a constitutional convention they would argue that it is ridiculous to even think that it would be entirely rewritten. The fact is, however, there is nothing to stop it from happening once the convention is convened, even if it is convened under the premise of being limited in scope.

It is ludicrous to think that the US Constitution is etched in stone and was written to address all possible situations that would arise in the future. It was not, as evidenced by the twenty-six amendments that have followed since ratification of the US Constitution. Therefore, in the interest of ensuring a more perfect democracy, with true equality of opportunity, there are some constitutional amendments that should be considered. Such amendments should only be considered by logical, reasoning people who would not have ulterior motives in mind. Any such amendments should be provided to meet the need for equality of opportunity for everyone. To ensure that the working class is treated fairly, the actions necessary to protect a decent standard of living for the working class and installing a Social Capitalist economic system must become constitutional amendments in order to attain a balanced, equitable democracy.

The US Constitution is silent on the economic system that is needed to perpetuate a democratic nation. This silence has given rise to many of the problems the nation faces today. Does this silence mean that we should add articles to the US Constitution to include economic principles as a guide for the economy of a democratic nation? The answer is yes! The addition of articles to address the issues needed to provide a fair and equitable economic system for everyone is needed. It is possible to enact legislation to address these issues, but legislation is more easily changed through partisan politics, which makes constitutional amendments a more permanent solution. A constitutional amendment to invoke a Social Capitalist economic system is a necessary component for the US Constitution.

Americans must be careful of the rhetoric that some would expound that the US Constitution is perfect and must not be altered. Individuals who have offered such rhetoric in the past usually flow with the tide. They are for an amendment if it is in their best interest, and stand on the perfection of the US Constitution when the amendment offered is not their personal desire. There are, however, issues that should be considered for a constitutional convention or as amendments if the opportunity arises. They should include variations of Franklin D. Roosevelt's "Economic Bill of Rights" and Senator Huey Long's "Share Our Wealth," and also:

1. Constitutionally provide that the economic system of the United States will be Social Capitalism for equality in economic opportunity for all through a three-party partnership of the working class, capitalists, and government regulation of the economy.

2. Ensure that the right of law-abiding citizens to own guns without fear of gun control, registration, or confiscation is affirmed for perpetuity.

3. Ensure that the rights of gays and lesbians are protected as with any citizen.

4. Provide for capital punishment only in cases where there is absolute guilt of murder as established through forensics, such as DNA testing.

5. Provide fair treatment of those injured by the acts of those convicted of a crime, as with victims' rights. If an individual convicted of a crime has caused loss or injury to another person, the perpetrator must be responsible for restitution for that loss or injury. A person incarcerated for a crime he or she did not commit, as evidenced by future action in the courts, must be compensated for the loss of liberty.

6. Provide for the term of service for a member of the House of Representatives be changed from two to four years.

7. Limit terms for the members of Congress to no more than one term of service to lessen abuse, minimize the advantages of incumbency, reduce posturing for reelection, and open the congressional service process to many other qualified individuals. (The intent was for turnover, not career politicians, without favor given to an incumbent to live and retire as a member of Congress, to draw perks and an unconscionable retirement at the expense of the taxpayers of the nation.)

8. Provide for an unbalanced budget as the product of a failed economic policy. (When the government has to provide for the underserved, unemployed, and indigent because capitalists are not required to provide for them, the result is an unbalanced budget.)

9. Provision for punishment of violent criminals and rehabilitation of nonviolent offenders must be incorporated into the justice system.

10. Provide that choice by the mother during the first trimester of pregnancy is in the U. S. Constitution. (The real issue is

religious or moral, not legal. However, there are those who would choose to impose their religious or moral views on others, which is exactly what the US Constitution forbids.)

11. Abolish the Electoral College and revert to the popular vote for selection of a president.

12. As a popular vote is established for selection of the president, the news media must be restrained from reporting election results prematurely. To provide equality in voter perception and participation, reporting results for presidential or congressional candidates must be held constitutionally until all the polls have closed nationwide.

13. Provide federal funding for candidates for the presidency and Congress and eliminate all private funding.

14. Provide for equal air time on media such as television, radio, and any other mass communication media for the final selected candidates for federal office.

15. Provide that the top two candidates receiving the most votes during a runoff election be placed on the ballot for any federal offices. (This ensures that, in keeping with a democracy, the elected official represents the majority.)

16. Provide that the right to vote is constitutionally guaranteed to every eligible citizen and that local officials must make every effort to assist voters to register to vote and then be able to vote in every election.

17. Establish the sanctity of voting in a democracy and ban the practice of cheating on elections with such things as voting

machines. Provide that voting machines or apparatuses of any kind must be capable of providing a paper trail in the event of a close vote count or recount.

18. Permanently establish tax rates at the rates in effect prior to the Reagan Economic Recovery Act of 1981.

19. Permanently establish the inheritance tax at the rate of 70 percent on estates. Provide an exemption of $5,000,000 with an annual increase of the exemption by the same index rate used for Social Security payments.

20. Establish that retirement security through employment benefits or Social Security for all Americans is guaranteed.

21. Establish that national universal health care for all Americans is guaranteed through a national Medicare/Medicaid program.

22. Establish that employers will be provided a tax credit per employee that is provided a living wage and living benefits.

23. Provide for a publicly funded college education or vocational training.

24. Provide for greater regulation of commodity production to stabilize prices.

25. Provide for greater regulation of the stock markets, banks, and other financial institutions. Separate commercial and investment banks, and make derivatives and interest rate swaps illegal.

26. Establish that a corporation is not a person and does not enjoy the rights of a person.

27. Establish tax structure to cap personal fortunes at ten thousand times the national median household income and limit annual income to two hundred fifty times the federal poverty level of a family of four.

28. Guarantee every working family an annual income of one-half the national median.

29. Guarantee every adult the right to at least a living wage and benefits.

30. Guarantee every American farmer the right to plant, raise, and sell his/her products without interference from multinational agricultural corporations.

31. Guarantee the right of every businessman, large and small, to trade in an atmosphere of freedom from unfair competition and domination by monopolies at home and abroad.

32. Guarantee the right of every family to an average standard home.

*"The punishment which the wise suffer who refuse
to take part in the government, is to live under the
government of worse men."*

—Plato

IV
SUMMARY

The reality in a democracy with a capitalism economy is that there are
two classes of people: capitalists and the noncapitalist working class,
or the "haves" and the "have-nots." The unfettered, unregulated,
laissez-faire, capitalist economic system as perpetrated for over two
hundred years in America has greatly benefited the capitalists while
leaving the noncapitalist working class as a tool or commodity of
the capitalists. Capitalists strive to minimize government and
government regulations, make little or no effort to enhance the
living standard of the working class, and, among other things,
constantly seek elimination of taxes and regulations on the wealthy.
The endeavors of the capitalists are in keeping with their perception
that under an unfettered capitalist economic system, the capitalists
are entitled to the fruits of their labor and there should not be any
government intervention, including taxation. Unfettered capitalism
must be replaced with Social Capitalism in order to provide fairness
in economic opportunity for all.

The working class in America deserves to benefit from that
which is perceived as being offered through America's statements,
proclamations, and democratic form of government. What the
working class want and deserve are decent jobs so their family can be

proud of them, living wages to be able to take care of their families, national health care to protect them from catastrophic events, and a retirement in dignity. With the wealth available in a democratic nation, this is not too much to ask. After all, it is repeatedly proven that the economy in a free society is fueled by working class labor. As the condition of the working class goes, so goes the economy. If the working class is underpaid, if their security is diminished, and if jobs are shipped out of the country in the name of profits for the greedy capitalists, the unfettered capitalist economy crumbles.

America needs a Social Capitalist economic system that will control greed and ensure that the working class is properly treated. The means to get a Social Capitalist economic system adopted in America is for all of the working class to get out and vote for the majority party candidates that have pledged to get rid of unfettered capitalism and replace it with Social Capitalism. This task can be difficult given that capitalists have taken numerous actions to cement their hold on the greed they enjoy under the unfettered capitalist economic system now in place. However, if the land of the free and home of the brave is going to survive for another two hundred and more years, the working class must install the statesmanlike leadership necessary to create an equitable economy for all.

Partisan politics have shown that the playing field will never be level with an unfettered capitalist economic system in place. Because the capitalists are in a minority in America, the capitalists, as the minority political party, will endeavor to entice the working class to vote with the capitalists by any and all tricks, propaganda, and rhetoric they can muster. Once the minority political party gains control of the government, all the efforts will be in favor of the capitalists and there will be nothing in favor of the working class. The working class as the majority political party must not be taken in by the propaganda and rhetoric of the minority party as they would be voting against their best interest in the long run.

Democracy is defined as government by the common people (working class), especially as the primary source of political power. Rule under a democracy is to be by the majority and the principles of social equality and respect for the individual within a community. Unfettered capitalism is at odds with democracy. If a capitalist minority party achieves control of the government, then the primary source of political power is not the majority but rather the minority of the people. The government as the "regulator" in seeing that there is a balance between capitalists and the working class is controlled by the capitalists. This again can create an economic imbalance as it has under recent minority party administrations. A balanced economic system is more likely from a democratic government of the majority. The majority party is not the party of accumulation, greed, deregulation, and privatization; it is the party of the working class. A democratically controlled government is more likely to maintain a working relationship between the three parties in a Social Capitalist economic system; capitalists, the working class, and the government. This would include seeing that capitalists pay their fair share through taxation for the right to accumulate reasonable wealth.

Unfettered capitalism as inherited and perpetuated from feudal times may have been accepted, or it may have been imposed on the working class. However, under a democracy of the people, by the people, and for the people, all classes of citizens must be acknowledged and treated fairly and equitably by the selected economic system. Such an economic system would be Social Capitalism: Social, to recognize and provide a decent standard of living for the majority working class, and Capitalism, to recognize and provide for the ingenuity and ambition of the minority capitalists, with the government as the regulator.

Unfettered capitalism as currently perpetrated provides capitalists with unfettered wealth accumulation. The trillions of dollars that are hoarded by capitalists without acknowledging the decent standard of living needed for the working class limit the governments options. While the working class has made it possible for the capitalists to amass their fortunes, they leave the government responsible to attempt to ensure a decent standard of living for noncapitalists through the enactment of social programs. Such social programs can only be funded with tax dollars, which the capitalists refuse to believe is their responsibility. To perpetrate their will on the nation, capitalists as the minority party take whatever measures are necessary to secure that candidates sympathetic to the capitalist cause are elected to the presidency, Congress, and state governments. The measures taken may be unethical, illegal, immoral, or any other means to achieve their end. Capitalists fear that a majority party president and Congress will eventually recognize the inequalities in the unfettered capitalism economic system and require them to give up some of their wealth through taxation to enhance the standard of living for the working class.

The working class must recognize that democracy is being systematically converted to a plutocracy by the capitalists and large corporations. A plutocracy is of, by, and for the wealthy, while a democracy is supposed to be of, by, and for the people, the working class. It is the votes of the working class supporting their majority party that can ensure that democracy lives on forever.

Democracy is defined as: "Rule by the majority, the common people, especially as the primary source of political power." However, when voting in a democracy is not mandated, then rule by the majority becomes rule by the majority of those voting, which is not the definition of a democracy. When a great number of the working class fails to vote or is prevented from voting, it can lead to rule by capitalists as in a plutocracy. Changes that could lead to greater voter participation could include the automatic registration of every citizen to vote after attaining a specific age similar to the requirement for a Social Security number, or voting by mail tracked through each individual's social security number to minimize fraud or abuse.

To achieve the greatest voter turnout in a democracy, certain conditions must be present within that democracy, including: a free press and unbiased news media that reports truthfully, opening the election process to all eligible citizens and not just the wealthy, a publicly educated electorate, and enforcement of election laws. Unfortunately, in America these conditions are not in place as they should be. The capitalists have orchestrated: to purchase and control the news media to use for their propaganda purposes, to make unlimited capitalist and corporate funding available to buy influence of political candidates who will support the capitalist agenda to the detriment of the working class, to push for the systematic privatization of the educational system for the purpose of invoking the capitalist educational agenda and profiteering from public education funds, and to obstruct the ability of the working class to register to vote or actually vote. In order to change these tactics, laws must be passed or changed or enforced. If the capitalists in control of the government will not voluntarily implement the necessary changes, the working class must gain control of the government by voting their interests and then implementing the necessary changes. This would require a massive effort to get great turnouts at the elections regardless of the obstacles. To achieve the changes needed in America, it's time the working class endorsed the need for change by becoming involved in the political process and voting.

The time to recognize that unfettered capitalism is inequitable and unfair and must be revised to Social Capitalism is now. Following is an agenda for accomplishing a change from unfettered capitalism to Social Capitalism, in which capitalists are held responsible for providing a fair standard of living to the working class. Democracy is not a spectator sport; every member of the working class must get involved in the political process and not become enablers to a plutocracy government.

An agenda to achieve a Social Capitalist economic system would be:

1. All eligible members of the working class get registered to vote and then vote their interests for majority party candidates in all elections.

2. Working class voters vote for candidates who acknowledge and support the working class and a change to a Social Capitalist economic system.

3. Once the majority party controls the presidency, Congress, and the vast majority of state governments, Congress initiates the constitutional changes listed in chapter 3, part 12.

Social Capitalism recognizes that with the privilege of private ownership of the means of production and distribution goes the social responsibility to ensure that every able-bodied member of the working class is employed or provided for at a living wage and benefits. Government facilitates full employment with incentives to the private sector. Only with the adoption of Social Capitalism will the potential exist for a statesmanlike democracy rather than the partisan politics that has evolved.

It is the working class that creates the capitalists' prosperity. It is government that is responsible for establishing parameters, controls, and regulations over capitalism. Currently, unfettered capitalism does not support the working class as equals under a democracy, but as a commodity (labor). This is part of the flaw in unfettered capitalism. The missing link in the unfettered capitalist economic system is the failure to require the capitalists to be socially responsible. Capitalism must provide for the needs of the working class as equals in the economy, not as a commodity like rice, sugar, or steel. The failure to recognize the economic system as a three-party partnership of the working class, capitalists, and the government has resulted in the gross inequalities in the economic system. The partnership under a Social Capitalist economic system must be an association working toward a common goal, not an association of adversaries and partisan politics.

In the early years of this nation, many of the working class were illiterate and unskilled. Perceiving the working class as a commodity fit the economists' models in a manner which would maintain an orderly unfettered capitalist economic system. Whether intentional or not, it has evolved this way, under the cloak of economic freedom, with the false promise that anyone may elevate to a higher social level under unfettered capitalism. Such a system has been conveniently rationalized and justified by economists and capitalists, but can no longer be justified. Today's working class is educated, skilled, and deserving to be included as equal partners in the economy. It is time to end the practice of treating the working class as a commodity and proceed on to the reality that virtually every able-bodied member of the working class is educated, intelligent, proud, and anxious to be an equal contributor in a Social Capitalist economy of a three-party partnership: the working class, government, and capitalists.

In a true democracy and equitable economic system, every employee should have a right to be proud of where he or she works. Every employee should be able to have his or her family be proud of him or her and where he or she works. Corporate and business administrations and management must be required to ensure that every employee can be proud of his or her employment, thus allowing the families to be proud also. The place to begin to allow the working class to be proud of their employment is with the adoption of a Social Capitalist economic system.

Since every member of the working class is educated and has a brain and intelligence, why, then, would a democracy persist with an economic system that unequally favors capitalists over the working class? If the existing system enables the capitalist rich to get richer and prevents the working class from a decent standard of living, where is the motivation for education, for involvement by the voters, for production, for reduced dependence on social programs, etc.? This tradition has mutually established a class separation that perpetuates injustices on the working class. Even Adam Smith, the proponent of modern capitalism, had the wisdom to acknowledge: "No society can surely be flourishing and happy, of which the far greater part of the members are poor and miserable." The economic system that addresses the needs of all citizens is Social Capitalism.

> *The minds of the working class cannot be throttled by a lack of participation in the economic process, and then be expected to provide progress, quality, productivity, growth, and entrepreneurship.*

Capitalists would still own the means of production and distribution, but the role of the working class would change and improve dramatically. No longer would the working class be considered a commodity, but rather a partner in the economy, a partner with the capitalists. As partners, the working class would have employment at a living wage and benefits under a government full employment policy. In addition, to facilitate a full employment policy, government would provide job creation and employment incentives to the capitalists or private sector to employ all able-bodied members of the working class at least at living wages and benefits. The job creation incentives would be implemented and controlled by government to facilitate full employment throughout the nation. Once the structure of Social Capitalism has been established, there would exist a truly democratic Social Capitalist economic system to export to emerging nations as the economic model for all the people in nations choosing a free democracy.

Without Social Capitalism, democracy will continue the downward path to corporate control as a plutocracy where government "of, by, and for" the people is replaced with "of, by, and for" the capitalists. Inquisitiveness and entrepreneurship of the human mind and spirit must be continued in a Social Capitalist economic system. Without Social Capitalism, capitalists will continually strive to retain unfettered capitalism by seeking control of the government. If capitalists retain control of the government, they will continue to pass legislation to enhance their power at the expense of the working class. This will continue until the working class gain control of the government and try to enhance the position of the working class through government programs, taxation on the wealthy, increased minimum wage, etc. As has happened in the past, so shall it continue in the future unless Social Capitalism is enacted.

The government must provide whatever incentives are necessary to the private sector capitalists and the working class to ensure that jobs are created for every able-bodied member of the working class. The noncapitalists must be entitled to employment at a living wage, living benefits, and with proper working conditions. Failure to move from an unfettered capitalist-dominated economic system to a recognized three-party partnership with an equitable Social Capitalist economic system for all will mutually condemn many of the working class to poverty and a life without hope.

It is recognized that capitalists blame government for the burden of mandated regulations. In turn, government blames business for acting in such a manner that regulations are necessary. The truth lies somewhere in the middle. Under a flawed unfettered capitalist economic system, businesses believe that government must stay out of the economic picture. In return, businesses and capitalists will do what is best for the country. The sad truth is that elite capitalists have no intention of doing what is best for the country. Rather, they will do what is best for capitalists under the practice of unfettered capitalism. Ask any economist why anyone starts a business and you will invariably get the answer, "to make a profit." The answer does not include "to provide a viable product or service," or "to provide a decent living wage and benefits to employees." This is a significant difference between unfettered capitalism and Social Capitalism. In the interest of the country and the working class, the government must be involved in the economy. As many businesses do not act in the best interest of the public, mandated regulations need to be enforced on those businesses. This reluctance by capitalists to address the needs of the working class and the government having to mandate regulation over the capitalists is exactly why Social Capitalism is necessary. Unfettered capitalism promotes a profit motive and greed, and does not include job creation at living wages and benefits, which requires government involvement with policies, laws, and regulations to ensure full employment, which capitalists won't do.

This makes the shortcomings of unfettered capitalism very clear and shows the need for Social Capitalism. With Social Capitalism in place, the capitalists, government, and working class will eventually work in harmony toward economic goals. Government regulations must be to assist economic growth that is in concert with full employment and economic output. Greed and social abuses would be replaced by social responsibility and cooperation. Owners, management, labor, and government would work out solutions to problems that would be socially, economically, and environmentally sound. Those companies that were still irresponsible would be more heavily regulated than those that uphold their social responsibility.

The problem is that with most regulation comes mandatory compliance and submission of paperwork. Small and even large businesses must spend countless nonproductive hours preparing and submitting such paperwork, or suffer the threat of government ramifications. This approach to business is necessitated by the adversarial relationship developed by a flawed capitalism economic system. If Social Capitalism were the standard, excessive regulations may not be necessary to control the "profits at all costs" capitalist mentality. Those businesses that conduct their activities in a responsible manner would require little or no regulation. What would be wrong with eliminating excessive paperwork for businesses that continually meet acceptable standards of operation? Mandatory submissions should be a means of control over those who would abuse the public and the public interest, not a means to thwart the efforts toward job creation and legitimate businesses. There has proven to be a great need for government oversight and monitoring of the actions of capitalists because of the tremendous profit drive and greed. This often clouds the thinking of capitalists to the point that concerns for the environment, safety, health, and employees are subordinated.

It is necessary to get out the vote. Vote for integrity, business sense, leadership, and statesmen/stateswomen in government who can and will get the message that there are victims whose needs have to be met with equal economic opportunity as with a Social Capitalist economic system. Only the power of the voter can make the difference that will provide equal economic opportunity and full employment for everyone, and minimize or eliminate the unemployed and underemployed victims of an unjust society.

To be the model for a Social Capitalism economic system, America itself must execute the changes necessary to provide such a system of equal economic opportunity in America. However, since changing to such a system will take time, emerging nations must not be led to believe that the existing American unfettered capitalist economic system is the best that democracy can be. It isn't, and it should not be presented as being the best system. Why subject new emerging nations to the same errors that have plagued the American economic system? Why not seize the opportunity to recognize that the existing American economic system isn't perfect? There have been gross oversights that should not be passed on in the economic systems that will be established in emerging democratic nations. If emerging economies are developed on such a false model as that existing in America, the systems will function, but they may succumb to the same pitfalls of inequality, racism, crime, poverty, and discrimination that strangle America today.

As the rest of the world looks to America for guidance in their efforts toward democracy, they must not be disappointed. If America exports the existing model of a democratic unfettered capitalism economic system, the rest of the world will be disappointed when they learn the truth. Capitalists dominate and control such a system, while the working class is left to the whims of the capitalists and the government that capitalists will put in place. This is wrong. Such a system, held to create equal opportunity for all under the disguise of equality under democracy, is wrong. Developing nations must be told that a true democracy provides opportunity for all the people. Every individual must be provided equal economic opportunity either as an employee of the government, as a capitalist owner of the means of production and distribution, or as the working class. Each economic partner must have equal protection in the area of jobs and opportunity. Each partner must be recognized as an equal in a Social Capitalist economic system, all of whom are necessary in order for the system to operate as a democracy of equitable economic opportunity.

APPENDIX A

DECLARATION OF INDEPENDENCE
IN CONGRESS, JULY 4, 1776

THE UNANIMOUS DECLARATION of the thirteen united
STATES OF AMERICA.

WHEN in the Course of human events, it becomes necessary for one people to dissolve the political bands which have connected them with another, and to assume among the powers of the earth, the separate and equal station to which the Laws of Nature and of Nature's God entitle them, a decent respect to the opinions of mankind requires that they should declare the causes which impel them to the separation.

We hold these truths to be self-evident, that all men are created equal, that they are endowed by their Creator with certain unalienable Rights, that among these are Life, Liberty and the pursuit of Happiness. That to secure these rights, Governments are instituted among Men, deriving their just powers from the consent of the governed. That whenever any Form of Government becomes destructive of these ends, it is the Right of the People to alter or to abolish it, and to institute new Government, laying its foundation on such principles, and organizing its powers in such form, as to them shall seem most likely to effect their Safety and Happiness. Prudence, indeed, will dictate that Governments long established should not be changed for light and transient causes; and accordingly all experience hath shewn, that mankind are more disposed to suffer, while evils are sufferable, than to right themselves by abolishing the forms to which they are accustomed. But when a long train of abuses and usurpations, pursuing invariably the same Object, evinces a design to reduce them under absolute Despotism, it is their right, it is their duty, to throw off such Government, and to provide new Guards for their future security. Such has been the patient sufferance of these Colonies; and such is now the necessity which constrains them to alter their former Systems of Government. The history of the present King of Great Britain is a history of repeated injuries and usurpations, all having in direct object the establishment of an absolute Tyranny over these States. To prove this, let Facts be submitted to a candid world:

He has refused his Assent to Laws, the most wholesome and necessary for the public good.

He has forbidden his Governors to pass Laws of immediate and pressing importance, unless suspended in their operation till his Assent should be obtained; and when so suspended, he has utterly neglected to attend to them.

He has refused to pass other Laws for the accommodation of large districts of people, unless those people would relinquish the right of Representation in the Legislature, a right inestimable to them and formidable to tyrants only.

He has called together legislative bodies at places unusual, uncomfortable, and distant from the depository of their public Records, for the sole purpose of fatiguing them into compliance with his measures.

He has dissolved Representative Houses repeatedly, for opposing with manly firmness his invasions on the rights of the people.

He has refused for a long time, after such dissolutions, to cause others to be elected; whereby the Legislative powers, incapable of Annihilation, have returned to the People at large for their exercise; the State remaining in the mean time exposed to all the dangers of invasion from without, and convulsions within.

He has endeavoured to prevent the population of these States; for that purpose obstructing the Laws for Naturalization of Foreigners; refusing to pass others to encourage their migrations hither, and raising the conditions of new Appropriations of Lands.

He has obstructed the Administration of Justice, by refusing his Assent to Laws for establishing Judiciary powers.

He has made Judges dependent on his Will alone, for the tenure of their offices, and the amount and payment of their salaries.

He has erected a multitude of New Offices, and sent hither swarms of Officers to harass our people, and eat out their substance.

He has kept among us, in times of peace, Standing Armies, without the Consent of our legislatures.

He has affected to render the Military independent of and superior to the Civil power.

He has combined with others to subject us to a jurisdiction foreign to our constitution, and unacknowledged by our laws; giving his Assent to their Acts of pretended Legislation:

For quartering large bodies of armed troops among us:

For protecting them, by a mock Trial, from punishment for any Murders which they should commit on the Inhabitants of these States:

For cutting off our Trade with all parts of the world:

For imposing Taxes on us without our Consent:

For depriving us in many cases of the benefits of Trial by Jury:

For transporting us beyond Seas to be tried for pretended offences:

For abolishing the free System of English Laws in a neighbouring Province, establishing therein an Arbitrary government, and enlarging its Boundaries so as to render it at once an example and fit instrument for introducing the same absolute rule into these Colonies:

For taking away our Charters, abolishing our most valuable Laws and altering fundamentally the Forms of our Governments:

For suspending our own Legislatures, and declaring themselves invested with power to legislate for us in all cases whatsoever.

He has abdicated Government here by declaring us out of his Protection and waging War against us.

He has plundered our seas, ravaged our Coasts, burnt our towns, and destroyed the lives of our people.

He is at this time transporting large Armies of foreign Mercenaries to complete the works of death, desolation and tyranny, already begun with circumstances of Cruelty & perfidy scarcely paralleled in the most barbarous ages, and totally unworthy the Head of a civilized nation.

He has constrained our fellow Citizens taken Captive on the high Seas to bear Arms against their Country, to become the executioners of their friends and Brethren, or to fall themselves by their Hands.

He has excited, domestic insurrections amongst us, and has endeavored to bring on the inhabitants of our frontiers, the merciless Indian Savages, whose known rule of warfare is an undistinguished destruction of all ages, sexes and conditions.

In every stage of these Oppressions We have Petitioned for Redress in the most humble terms. Our repeated Petitions have been answered only by repeated injury. A Prince, whose character is thus marked by every act which may define a Tyrant, is unfit to be the ruler of a free people.

Nor have We been wanting in attentions to our British brethren. We have warned them from time to time of attempts by their legislature to extend an unwarrantable jurisdiction over us. We have reminded them of the circumstances of our emigration and settlement here. We have appealed to their native justice and magnanimity, and we have conjured them by the ties of our common kindred to disavow these usurpations, which would inevitably interrupt our connections and correspondence. They too have been deaf to the voice of justice and of consanguinity. We must, therefore, acquiesce in the necessity, which denounces our Separation, and hold them, as we hold the rest of mankind, Enemies in War, in Peace Friends.

WE, THEREFORE the Representatives of the UNITED STATES OF AMERICA, in General Congress, Assembled, appealing to the Supreme Judge of the world for the rectitude of our intentions, do, in the Name and by Authority of the good People of these Colonies, solemnly publish and declare, That these United Colonies are and of Right ought to be FREE AND INDEPENDENT STATES; that they are Absolved from all Allegiance to the British Crown, and that all political connection between them and the State of Great Britain, is and ought to be totally dissolved; and that as Free and Independent States, they have full Power to levy War, conclude Peace, contract Alliances, establish Commerce, and to do all other Acts and Things which Independent states may of right do.

AND for the support of this Declaration, with a firm reliance on the protection of divine Providence, we mutually pledge to each other our Lives, our Fortunes and our sacred Honor.

APPENDIX B

Constitution of the United States of America

Preamble

We the people of the United States, in Order to form a more perfect Union, establish Justice, insure domestic Tranquility, provide for the common defence, promote the general Welfare, and secure the Blessings of Liberty to ourselves and our posterity, do ordain and establish this Constitution for the United States of America.

Article I

Section 1.   All legislative Powers herein granted shall be vested in a Congress of the United States, which shall consist of a Senate and House of Representatives.

Section 2.   The House of Representatives shall be composed of Members chosen every second Year by the People of the several States, and the Electors in each State shall have the Qualifications requisite for Electors of the most numerous Branch of the State Legislature.

No person shall be a Representative who shall not have attained to the Age of twenty five Years, and been seven Years a Citizen of the United States, and who shall not, when elected, be an Inhabitant of that State in which he shall be chosen.

Representatives and direct [Taxes] (1) shall be apportioned among the several States which may be included within this Union, according to their respective Numbers [which shall be determined by adding to the whole Number of free Persons, including those bound to Service for a Term of Years, and excluding Indians not taxed, three fifths of all other Persons]. (2) The actual Enumeration shall be made within three Years after the first Meeting of the Congress of the United States, and within every subsequent Term of ten Years, in such Manner as they shall by law direct. The Number of Representatives shall not exceed one for every thirty Thousand, but each State shall have at Least one Representative; and until such enumeration shall be made, the State of New Hampshire shall be entitled to chuse three, Massachusetts eight, Rhode Island and Providence Plantations one, Connecticut five, New-York six, New Jersey four, Pennsylvania eight, Delaware one, Maryland six, Virginia ten, North Carolina five, South Carolina five, and Georgia three.

When vacancies happen in the Representation from any State, the Executive Authority thereof shall issue Writs of Election to fill such Vacancies.

The House of Representatives shall chuse their Speaker and other Officers; and shall have the sole Power of Impeachment.

Section 3.   The Senate of the United States shall be composed of Two Senators from each State [chosen by the legislature thereof], (3) for six Years; and each Senator shall have one Vote.

Immediately after they shall be assembled in Consequence of the first Election, they shall be divided as equally as may be into three Classes. The Seats of the Senators of the first Class shall be vacated at the Expiration of the second Year, of the second Class at the Expiration of the fourth Year, and of the third Class at the Expiration of the sixth Year, so that one third may be chosen every second Year [and if Vacancies happen by Resignation, or otherwise, during the Recess of the Legislature of any State, the Executive thereof may make temporary Appointments until the next Meeting of the Legislature, which shall then fill such Vacancies.] (4)

No Person shall be a Senator who shall not have attained to the Age of thirty Years, and been nine Years a Citizen of the United States, and who shall not, when elected, be an Inhabitant of that State for which he shall be chosen.

The Vice President of the United States shall be President of the Senate, but shall have no Vote, unless they be equally divided.

The Senate shall chuse their other Officers, and also a President pro tempore, in the Absence of the Vice President, or when he shall exercise the Office of the President of the United States.

The Senate shall have sole Power to try all Impeachments. When sitting for that Purpose, they shall be on Oath or Affirmation. When the President of the United States is tried, the Chief Justice shall preside: And no Person shall be convicted without the Concurrence of two thirds of the Members present.

Judgment in Cases of Impeachment shall not extend further than to removal from Office, and disqualification to hold and enjoy any Office of honor, Trust or Profit under the United States; but the Party convicted shall nevertheless be liable and subject to Indictment, Trail, Judgment and Punishment, according to Law.

Section 4.   The Times, Places and Manner of holding Elections for Senators and Representatives, shall be prescribed in each State by the Legislature thereof; but Congress may at any time by Law make or alter such Regulations, except as to the Places of chusing Senators.

[The Congress shall assemble at least once in every Year, and such Meeting shall be on the first Monday in December, unless they shall by Law appoint a different Day.] (5)

Section 5.   Each house shall be the Judge of the Elections, Returns and Qualifications of its own Members, and a Majority of each shall constitute a Quorum to do Business; but a smaller Number may adjourn from day to day, and may be authorized to compel the Attendance of absent Members, in such Manner, and under such Penalties as each House may provide.

Each House may determine the Rules of its Proceedings, punish its Members for disorderly Behaviour, and, with the Concurrence of two thirds, expel a Member.

Each House shall keep a Journal of its Proceedings, and from time to time publish the same, excepting such Parts as may in their Judgment require Secrecy; and the Yeas and Nays of the Members of either House on any question shall, at the Desire of one fifth of those present, be entered on the Journal.

Neither House, during the Session of Congress, shall, without the Consent of the other, adjourn for more than three days, nor to any other Place than that in which the two Houses shall be sitting.

Section 6.   The Senators and Representatives shall receive a Compensation for their Services, to be ascertained by Law, and paid out of the Treasury of the United States. They shall in all cases, except Treason, Felony and Breach of the Peace, be privileged from Arrest during their Attendance at the Session of their respective Houses, and in going to and returning from the same; and for any Speech or Debate in either House, they shall not be questioned in any other place.

No Senator or Representative shall, during the Time for which he was elected, be appointed to any civil Office under the Authority of the United States, which shall have been created, or the Emoluments whereof shall have been increased during such time; and no Person holding any Office under the United States, shall be a member of either house during his Continuance in Office.

Section 7.   All Bills for raising Revenue shall originate in the House of Representatives; but the Senate may propose or concur with Amendments as on other Bills.

Every Bill which shall have passed the House of Representatives and the Senate, shall, before it become a Law, be presented to the President of the United States; If he approves he shall sign it, but if not he shall return it, with his Objections to that House in which it shall have originated, who shall enter the Objections at large on their Journal, and proceed to reconsider it. If after such Reconsideration two thirds of that House shall agree to pass the Bill, it shall be sent, together with the Objections, to the other House, by which it shall likewise be reconsidered, and if approved by two thirds of that House, it shall become a Law. But in all such Cases the Votes of both Houses shall be determined by yeas and Nays, and the Names of the Persons voting for and against the Bill shall be entered on the Journal of each House respectively. If any Bill shall not be returned by the President within ten Days (Sundays excepted) after it shall have been presented to him, the Same shall be a Law, in like Manner as if he had signed it, unless the Congress by their Adjournment prevent its Return, in which Case it shall not be a Law.

Every Order, Resolution, or Vote to which the Concurrence of the Senate and House of Representatives may be necessary (except on a question of Adjournment) shall be presented to the President of the United States; and before the Same shall take Effect, shall be approved by him, or being disapproved by him, shall be repassed by two thirds of the Senate and House of Representatives, according to the Rules and Limitations prescribed in the Case of a Bill.

Section 8.   The Congress shall have Power To lay and collect Taxes, Duties, Imposts and Excises, to pay the Debts and provide for the common Defense and general Welfare of the United States; but all Duties, Imposts and Excises shall be uniform throughout the United States;

To borrow Money on the credit of the United States;

To regulate Commerce with foreign nations, and among the several States, and with the Indian Tribes;

To establish a uniform Rule of Naturalization, and uniform Laws on the subject of Bankruptcies throughout the United States;

To coin Money, regulate the Value thereof, and of foreign Coin, and fix the Standard of Weights and Measures;

To provide for the Punishment of counterfeiting the Securities and current Coin of the United States;

To establish Post Offices and post Roads;

To promote the Progress of Science and useful Arts, by securing for limited Times to Authors and Inventors the exclusive Right to their respective Writings and Discoveries;

To constitute Tribunals inferior to the Supreme Court;

To define and punish Piracies and Felonies committed on the high Seas, and Offenses against the Law of Nations;

To declare War, grant Letters of Marque and Reprisal, and make Rules concerning Captures on Land and Water;

To raise and support Armies, but no Appropriation of Money to that Use shall be for a longer Term than two Years;

To provide and maintain a Navy;

To make Rules for the Government and Regulation of the land and naval Forces;

To provide for calling forth the Militia to execute the Laws of the Union, suppress Insurrections and repel Invasions;

To provide for organizing, arming, and disciplining the Militia, and for governing such Part of them as may be employed in the Service of the United States, reserving to the States respectively, the Appointment of the Officers, and the Authority of training the Militia according to the discipline prescribed by Congress;

To exercise exclusive legislation in all Cases whatsoever, over such District (not exceeding ten miles square) as may, by Cession of particular States, and the Acceptance of Congress, become the Seat of the Government of the United States, and to exercise like Authority over all Places purchased by the Consent of the Legislature of the State in which the Same shall be, for the Erection of Forts, Magazines, Arsenals, dock-Yards, and other needful Buildings;

And

To make all Laws which shall be necessary and proper for carrying into Execution the foregoing Powers, and all other Powers vested by this Constitution in the Government of the United States, or in any Department or Officer thereof.

Section 9.
The Migration or Importation of such Persons as any of the States now existing shall think proper to admit, shall not be prohibited by the Congress prior to the Year one thousand eight hundred and eight, but a Tax or duty may be imposed on such Importation, not exceeding ten dollars for each Person.

The Privilege of the Writ of Habeas Corpus shall not be suspended, unless when in cases of Rebellion or Invasion the public Safety may require it.

No Bill of Attainer or ex post facto law shall be passed.

[No Capitation, or other direct, Tax shall be laid, unless in Proportion to the Census or Enumeration herein before directed to be taken.] (6)

No Tax or Duty shall be laid on Articles exported from any State.

No Preference shall be given by any Regulation of Commerce or Revenue to the Ports of one State over those of another; nor shall Vessels bound to, or from, one State, be obliged to enter, clear, or pay Duties in another.

No Money shall be drawn from the Treasury, but in Consequence of Appropriations made by Law; and a regular Statement and Account of the Receipts and Expenditures of all public Money shall be published from time to time.

No Title of Nobility shall be granted by the United States; And no Person holding any Office of Profit or Trust under them, shall, without the Consent of the Congress, accept of any present, Emolument, Office, or Title, of any kind whatever, from any King, Prince, or foreign State.

Section 10.   No state shall enter into any Treaty, Alliance, or Confederation; grant Letters of Marque and Reprisal; coin Money; emit Bills of Credit; make any Thing but gold and silver Coin a Tender in Payment of Debts; pass any Bill of Attainer, ex post facto Law, or Law impairing the Obligation of Contracts, or grant any Title of Nobility.

No State shall, without the Consent of the Congress, lay any imposts or Duties on Imports or Exports, except what may be absolutely necessary for executing its inspection Laws; and the net Produce of all Duties and Imposts, laid by any State on Imports or Exports, shall be for the Use of the Treasury of the United States;

and all such Laws shall be subject to the Revision and Control of the Congress.

No State shall, without the Consent of Congress, lay and Duty of Tonnage, keep Troops, or Ships of War in time of Peace, enter into any Agreement or Compact with another State, or foreign Power or engage in War, unless actually invaded, or in such imminent Danger as will not admit of delay.

Article II

Section 1.   The executive Power shall be vested in a President of the United States of America. He shall hold his Office during the Term of four Years, and, together with the Vice President, chosen for the Same Term, be elected, as follows.

Each State shall appoint, in such Manner as the Legislature thereof may direct, a Number of Electors, equal to the whole number of Senators and Representatives to which the State may be entitled in the Congress; but no Senator or Representative, or Person holding an Office of Trust or Profit under the United States, shall be appointed an Elector.

[The Electors shall meet in their respective States, and vote by Ballot for two persons of whom one at least shall not be an Inhabitant of the same State with themselves. And they shall make a List of all the Persons voted for, and of the Number of Votes for each; which List they shall sign and certify, and transmit sealed to the Seat of the Government of the United States, directed to the President of the Senate. The President of the Senate shall, in the Presence of the Senate and House of Representatives, open all the Certificates, and the Votes shall then be counted. The Person having the greatest Number of Votes shall be the President, if such Number be a Majority of the whole Number of Electors appointed; and if there be more than one who have such Majority, and have an equal Number of Votes, then the House of Representatives shall immediately chuse by Ballot one of them for President; and if no Person have a Majority, then from the five highest on the List the said House shall in like Manner chuse the President. But in chusing the President, the Votes shall be taken by States, the Representation from each State having one vote; A quorum for this Purpose shall consist of a Member or Members from two thirds of the States, and a Majority of all the States shall be necessary to a Choice. In every Case, after the Choice of the President, the Person having the greatest Number of Votes of the Electors shall be the Vice President. But if there should remain two or more who have equal Votes, the Senate shall chuse from them by Ballot the Vice President.] (7)

The Congress may determine the Time of chusing the Electors, and the Day on which they shall give their Votes; which Day shall be the same throughout the United States.

No Person except a natural born Citizen, or a Citizen of the United States, at the time of the Adoption of this Constitution, shall be eligible to the Office of President; neither shall any Person be eligible to that Office who shall not have attained to the Age of thirty five Years, and been fourteen Years a Resident within the United States.

[In Case of the Removal of the President from Office, or of his Death, Resignation, or Inability to discharge the Powers and Duties of the said Office, the same shall devolve on the Vice President, and the Congress may by Law provide for the Case of Removal, Death, Resignation or Inability, both of the President and Vice President, declaring what Officer shall then act as President, and such Officer shall act accordingly, until the Disability be removed, or a President shall be elected.] (8)

The President shall, at stated Times, receive for his Services, a Compensation, which shall neither be encreased nor diminished during the Period for which he shall have been elected, and he shall not receive within that Period any other Emolument from the United States, or any of them.

Before he enter on the Execution of his Office, he shall take the following Oath of Affirmation: —"I do solemnly swear (or affirm) that I will faithfully execute the Office of President of the United States, and will to the best of my Ability, preserve, protect and defend the Constitution of the United States."

Section 2.   The President shall be Commander in Chief of the Army and Navy of the United States, and of the Militia of the several States, when called into the actual Service of the United States; he may require the Opinion, in writing, of the principle Officer in each of the executive

Departments, upon any Subject relating to the Duties of their respective Offices, and he shall have Power to grant Reprieves and Pardons for Offenses against the United States, except in Cases of Impeachment.

He shall have Power, by and with the Advice and Consent of the Senate, to make Treaties, provided two thirds of the Senators present concur; and he shall nominate, and by and with the Advice and Consent of the Senate, shall appoint Ambassadors, other public Ministers and Consuls, Judges of the supreme Court, and all other Officers of the United States, whose Appointments are not herein otherwise provided for, and which shall be established by law; but the Congress may by Law vest the Appointment of such inferior Officers, as they think proper, in the President alone, in the Courts of Law, or in the Heads of Departments.

The President shall have Power to fill up all Vacancies that may happen during the Recess of the Senate, by granting Commissions which shall expire at the end of their next Session.

Section 3.   He shall from time to time give to the Congress Information of the State of the Union, and recommend to their Consideration such Measures as he shall judge necessary and expedient; he may, on extraordinary Occasions, convene both Houses, or either of them, and in Case of Disagreement between them, with Respect to the Time of Adjournment, he may adjourn them to such Time as he shall think proper; he shall receive Ambassadors and other public Ministers; he shall take Care that the Laws be faithfully executed, and shall Commission all the Officers of the United States.

Section 4.   The President, Vice President and all civil Officers of the United States, shall be removed from Office on Impeachment for, and Conviction of, Treason, Bribery, or other high Crimes and Misdemeanors.

Article III

Section 1.   The judicial Power of the United States, shall be vested in one Supreme Court, and in such inferior Courts as the Congress may from time to time ordain and establish. The Judges, both of the supreme and inferior Courts, shall hold their Offices during good Behaviour, and shall, at stated Times, receive for their Services, a Compensation, which shall not be diminished during their Continuance in Office.

Section 2.   The judicial Power shall extend to all Cases, in Law and Equity, arising under this Constitution, the Laws of the United States, and Treaties made, or which shall be made, under their Authority; —to all Cases affecting Ambassadors, other public Ministers and Consuls; — to all Cases of admiralty and maritime Jurisdiction; — to Controversies to which the United States shall be a Party; —to Controversies between two or more States; [—between a State and Citizens of another State;] (9) —between Citizens of different States, —between Citizens of the same State claiming Lands under Grants of different States, [and between a state, or the Citizens thereof, and foreign States, Citizens or Subjects.] (10)

In all Cases affecting Ambassadors, other public Ministers and Consuls, and those in which a State shall be Party, the Supreme Court shall have original Jurisdiction. In all other Cases before mentioned, the Supreme Court shall have appellate Jurisdiction, both as to Law and Fact, with such Exceptions, and under such Regulations as the Congress shall make.

The Trial of all Crimes, except in Cases of Impeachment, shall be by Jury; and such Trial shall be held in the State where the said Crimes shall have been committed; but when not committed within any State, the Trial shall be at such Place or Places as the Congress may by law have directed.

Section 3.   Treason against the United States, shall consist only in levying War against them, or in adhering to their Enemies, giving them Aid and Comfort. No Person shall be convicted of Treason unless on the Testimony of two Witnesses to the same overt Act, or on Confession in open Court.

The Congress shall have Power to declare the Punishment of Treason, but no Attainder of Treason shall work Corruption of Blood, or Forfeiture except during the Life of the Person attainted.

Article IV

Section 1.   Full Faith and Credit shall be given in each State to the public Acts, Records, and judicial Proceedings of every other State. And the Congress may by general Laws prescribe the Manner in which such Acts, Records and Proceedings shall be proved, and the Effect thereof.

Section 2.   The Citizens of each State shall be entitled to all Privileges and Immunities of Citizens in the several States.

A Person charged in any State with Treason, Felony, or other Crime, who shall flee from Justice, and be found in another State, shall on Demand of the executive Authority of the State from which he fled, be delivered up, to be removed to the State having jurisdiction of the Crime.

[No Person held to Service or Labour in one State under the Laws thereof, escaping into another, shall, in Consequence of any Law or Regulation therein, be discharged from such Service or Labour, but shall be delivered up on Claim of the Party to whom such Service or Labour may be due.] (11)

Section 3.   New States may be admitted by the Congress into this Union; but no new State shall be formed or erected within the Jurisdiction of any other State; nor any State be formed by the Junction of two or more States, or Parts of States, without the Consent of the Legislatures of the States concerned as well as of the Congress.

The Congress shall have Power to dispose of and make all needful Rules and Regulations respecting the Territory or other Property belonging to the United States; and nothing in this Constitution shall be so construed as to Prejudice any Claimes of the United States, or of any particular State.

Section 4.   The United States shall guarantee to every State in this Union a Republican Form of Government, and shall protect each of them against Invasion, and on Application of the Legislature, or of the Executive (when the Legislature cannot be convened) against domestic Violence.

Article V

The Congress, whenever two thirds of both Houses shall deem it necessary, shall propose Amendments to this Constitution, or on the Application of the Legislatures of two thirds of the several States, shall call a Convention for proposing Amendments, which, in either Case, shall be valid to all Intents and Purposes, as Part of this Constitution, when ratifies by the Legislatures of three fourths of the several States, or by Conventions in three fourths thereof, as the one or the other Mode of Ratification may be proposed by the Congress; Provided that no Amendment which may be made prior to the Year One thousand eight hundred and eight shall in any Manner affect the first and fourth Clauses in the Ninth Section of the first Article; and that no State, without its Consent, shall be deprived of its equal Suffrage in the Senate.

Article VI

All Debts contracted and Engagements entered into, before the Adoption of this Constitution, shall be as valid against the United States under this Constitution, as under the Confederation.

This Constitution, and the laws of the United States which shall be made in Pursuance thereof; and all Treaties made, or which shall be made, under the Authority of the United States, shall be the supreme Law of the Land; and the Judges in every State shall be bound thereby, any Thing in the Constitution or Laws of any State to the Contrary notwithstanding.

The Senators and Representatives before mentioned, and the Members of the several State Legislatures, and all executive and judicial Officers, both of the United States and of the several States, shall be bound by Oath or Affirmation, to support this Constitution: but no religious Test shall ever be required as a Qualification to any Office or public Trust under the United States.

Article VII

The Ratification of the Conventions of nine States, shall be sufficient for the Establishment of this Constitution between the States so ratifying the Same.

Done in Convention by the Unanimous Consent of the States present the Seventeenth Day of September in the Year of our Lord one thousand seven hundred and Eighty seven and of the Independence of the United States of America the Twelfth. IN WITNESS whereof we have hereunto subscribed our Names,

Go. WASHINGTON

Pres't. and deputy from Virginia

Attest

WILLIAM JACKSON

Secretary

Bill of Rights

The Ten Original Amendments

(Ratified December 15, 1791)

Articles in addition to, and amendment of the Constitution of the United States of America, proposed by Congress and ratified by the Legislatures of the several states, pursuant to the Fifth Article of the original Constitution.

Amendment I

Congress shall make no law respecting an establishment of religion, or prohibiting the free exercise thereof; or abridging the freedom of speech, or of the press; or the right of the people peaceably to assemble, and to petition the Government for a redress of grievances.

Amendment II

A well regulated militia, being necessary to the security of a free State, the right of the people to keep and bear arms, shall not be infringed.

Amendment III

No Soldier shall, in time of peace be quartered in any house, without the consent of the owner, nor in time of war, but in a manner to be prescribed by law.

Amendment IV

The right of the people to be secure in their persons, houses, papers, and effects, against unreasonable searches and seizures, shall not be violated, and no warrants shall issue, but upon probable cause, supported by oath or affirmation, and particularly describing the place to be searched, and the persons or things to be seized.

Amendment V

No person shall be held to answer for a capital, or otherwise infamous crime, unless on a presentment or indictment of a Grand Jury, except in cases arising in the land or naval forces, or in the militia, when in actual service in time of war or public danger; nor shall any person be subject for the same offence to be twice put in jeopardy of life or limb; nor shall be compelled in any criminal case to be a witness against himself, nor be deprived of life, liberty, or property, without due process of law; nor shall private property be taken for public use, without just compensation.

Amendment VI

In all criminal prosecutions, the accused shall enjoy the right to a speedy and public trial, by an impartial jury of the State and district wherein the crime shall have been committed, which district shall have been previously ascertained by law, and to be informed of the nature and cause of the accusation; to be confronted with the witnesses against him; to have compulsory process for obtaining witnesses in his favor, and to have the assistance of counsel for his defence.

Amendment VII

In Suits at common law, where the value in controversy shall exceed twenty dollars, the right of trial by jury shall be preserved, and no fact tried by a jury, shall be otherwise reexamined in any Court of the United States, than according to the rules of common law.

Amendment VIII

Excessive bail shall not be required, nor excessive fines imposed, nor cruel and unusual punishment inflicted.

Amendment IX

The enumeration in the Constitution, of certain rights, shall not be construed to deny or disparage others retained by the people.

Amendment X

The powers not delegated to the United States by the Constitution, nor prohibited by it to the States, are reserved to the States respectively, or to the people.

Amendment XI (Ratified February 7, 1795)

The Judicial power of the United States shall not be construed to extend to any suit in law or equity, commenced or prosecuted against one of the United States by Citizens of another State, or by Citizens or Subjects of any Foreign State.

Amendment XII (Ratified June 15, 1804)

The Electors shall meet in their respective states, and vote by ballot for President and Vice-President, one of whom, at least, shall not be an inhabitant of the same state with themselves; they shall name in their ballots the person voted for as President, and in distinct ballots the person voted for as Vice-President, and they shall make distinct lists of all persons voted for as President, and of all persons voted for as Vice-President, and of the number of votes for each, which lists they shall sign and certify, and transmit sealed to the seat of the government of the United States, directed to the President of the Senate; —The President of the Senate shall, in the presence of the Senate and House of Representatives, open all the certificates and the votes shall then be counted; —The person having the greatest number of votes for President, shall be the President, if such number be a majority of the whole number of Electors appointed; and if no person have such majority, then from the persons having the highest numbers not exceeding three on the list of those voted for as President, the House of Representatives shall choose immediately, by ballot, the President. But in choosing the President, the votes shall be taken by states, the representation from each state having one vote; a quorum for this purpose shall consist of a member or members from two-thirds of the states, and a majority of all the states shall be necessary to a choice. [And if the House of Representative shall not choose a President whenever the right of choice shall devolve upon them, before the fourth day of March next following, then the Vice-President shall act as President, as in the case of the death or other constitutional disability of the President.] (12) —The Person having the greatest number of votes as Vice-President, shall be the Vice-President, if such number be a majority of the whole number of Electors appointed, and if no person have a majority, then from the two highest numbers on the list, the Senate shall choose the Vice-President; a quorum for the purpose shall consist of two-thirds of the whole number of Senators, and a majority of the whole number shall be necessary to a choice. But no person constitutionally ineligible to the office of President shall be eligible to that of Vice-President of the United States.

Amendment XIII (Ratified December 6, 1865)

Section 1. Neither slavery nor involuntary servitude, except as a punishment for crime whereof the party shall have been duly convicted, shall exist within the United States, or any place subject to their jurisdiction.

Section 2.   Congress shall have power to enforce this article by appropriate legislation.

Amendment XIV (Ratified July 9, 1868)

Section 1.   All persons born or naturalized in the United States, and subject to the jurisdiction thereof, are citizens of the United States and of the State wherein they reside. No State shall make or enforce any law which shall abridge the privileges or immunities of citizens of the United States; nor shall any State deprive any person of life, liberty, or property, without due process of law; nor deny to any person within its jurisdiction the equal protection of the laws.

Section 2.   Representatives shall be apportioned among the several States according to their respective numbers, counting the whole number of persons in each State, excluding Indians not taxed. But when the right to vote at any election for the choice of electors for President and Vice President of the United States, Representatives in Congress, the Executive and Judicial officers of a State, or the members of the Legislature thereof, is denied to any of the male inhabitants of such State, being [twenty-one] (13) years of age, and citizens of the United States, or in any way abridged, except for participation in rebellion, or other crime, the basis of representation therein shall be reduced in the proportion which the number of such male citizens shall bear to the whole number of male citizens twenty-one years of age in such State.

Section 3.   No person shall be a Senator or Representative in Congress, or elector of President and Vice President, or hold any office, civil or military, under the United States, or under any State, who having previously taken an oath, as a member of Congress, or as an officer of the United States, or as a member of any State Legislature, or as an executive or judicial officer of any State, to support the Constitution of the United States, shall have engaged in insurrection or rebellion against the same, or given aid or comfort to the enemies thereof. But Congress may by a vote of two-thirds of each House, remove such disability.

Section 4.   The validity of the public debt of the United States, authorized by law, including debts incurred for payment of pensions and bounties for services in suppressing insurrection or rebellion, shall not be questioned. But neither the United States nor any State shall assume or pay any debt or obligation incurred in aid of insurrection or rebellion against the United States, or any claim for the loss or emancipation of any slave, but all such debts, obligations and claims shall be held illegal and void.

Section 5.   The Congress shall have power to enforce, by appropriate legislation, the provisions of this article.

Amendment XV (Ratified February 3, 1870)

Section 1.   The right of citizens of the United States to vote shall not be denied or abridged by the United States or by any State on account of race, color, or previous condition of servitude.

Section 2.   The Congress shall have power to enforce this article by appropriate legislation.

Amendment XVI (Ratified February 3, 1913)

The Congress shall have power to lay and collect taxes on incomes, from whatever source derived, without apportionment among the several States, and without regard to any census or enumeration.

Amendment XVII (Ratified April 8, 1913)

The Senate of the United States shall be composed of two Senators from each State, elected by the people thereof, for six years; and each Senator shall have one vote. The electors in each State shall have the qualifications requisite for electors of the most numerous branch of the State Legislatures.

When vacancies happen in the representation of any State in the Senate, the executive authority of such State shall issue writs of election to fill such vacancies: Provided, that the legislature of any State may empower the executive thereof to make temporary appointments until the people fill the vacancies by election as the legislature may direct.

This amendment shall not be so construed as to affect the election or term of any Senator chosen before it becomes valid as part of the Constitution.

Amendment XVIII (Ratified January 16, 1919) (14)

Section 1.   After one year from the ratification of this article the manufacture, sale, or transportation of intoxicating liquors within, the importation thereof into, or the exportation thereof from the United States and all territory subject to the jurisdiction thereof for beverage purposes is hereby prohibited.

Section 2.   The Congress and the several States shall have concurrent power to enforce this article by appropriate legislation.

Section 3.   This article shall be inoperative unless it shall have been ratified as an amendment to the Constitution by the legislatures of the several States, as provided in the Constitution, within seven years from the date of the submission hereof to the States by the Congress.

Amendment XIX (Ratified August 18, 1920)

The right of citizens of the United States to vote shall not be denied or abridged by the United States or by any State on account of sex.

Congress shall have power to enforce this article by appropriate legislation.

Amendment XX (Ratified January 23, 1933)

Section 1.   The terms of the President and Vice President shall end at noon on the 20th day of January, and the terms of Senators and Representatives at noon on the 3rd day of January, of the years in which such terms would have ended if this article had not been ratified, and the terms of their successors shall then begin.

Section 2.   The Congress shall assemble at least once in every year, and such meeting shall begin at noon on the 3rd day of January, unless they shall by law appoint a different day.

Section 3.   If, at the time fixed for the beginning of the term of the President, the President elect shall have died, the Vice

President elect shall become President. If a President shall not have been chosen before the time fixed for the beginning of his term, or if the President elect shall have failed to qualify, then the Vice President elect shall act as President until a President shall have qualified; and the Congress may by law provide for the case wherein neither a President elect nor a Vice President elect shall have qualified, declaring who shall then act as President, or the manner in which one who is to act shall be selected, and such person shall act accordingly until a President or Vice President shall have qualified.

Section 4.   The Congress may by law provide for the case of the death of any of the persons from whom the House of Representatives may choose a President whenever the rights of choice shall have devolved upon them, and for the case of the death of any of the persons from whom the Senate may choose a Vice President whenever the right of choice shall have devolved upon them.

Section 5.   Sections 1 and 2 shall take effect on the 15th day of October following ratification of this article.

Section 6.   This article shall be inoperative unless it shall have been ratified as an amendment to the Constitution by the legislatures of three-fourths of the several States within seven years from the date of its submission.

Amendment XXI (Ratified December 5, 1933)

Section 1.   The eighteenth article of amendment to the Constitution of the United States is hereby repealed.

Section 2. The transportation or importation into any State, Territory, or possession of the United States for delivery or use therein of intoxicating liquors, in violation of the laws thereof, is hereby prohibited.

Section 3. This article shall be inoperative unless it shall have been ratified as an amendment to the Constitution by conventions in the several States, as provided in the Constitution, within seven years from the date of the submission hereof to the States by the Congress.

Amendment XXII (Ratified February 27, 1951)

No person shall be elected to the office of the President more than twice, and no person who has held the office of President, or acted as President, for more than two years of a term to which some other person was elected President shall be elected to the office of the President more than once. But this Article shall not apply to any person holding the office of President when this Article was proposed by the Congress, and shall not prevent any person who may be holding the office of President, or acting as President, during the term within which this Article becomes Operative from holding the office of President or acting as President during the remainder of such term.

Amendment XXIII (Ratified March 29, 1961)

Section 1. The District constituting the seat of Government of the United States shall appoint in such manner as the Congress may direct:

A number of electors of President and Vice President equal to the whole number of Senators and

Representatives in Congress to which the District would be entitled if it were a State, but in no event more than the least populous State; they shall be in addition to those appointed by the States, but they shall be considered, for the purposes of the election of President and Vice President, to be electors appointed by a State; and they shall meet in the District and perform such duties as provided by the twelfth article of amendment.

Section 2.   The Congress shall have power to enforce this article by appropriate legislation.

Amendment XXIV (Ratified January 23, 1964)

Section 1.   The right of citizens of the United States to vote in any primary or other election for President or Vice President, for electors for President or Vice President, or for Senator or Representative in Congress, shall not be denied or abridged by the United States or any State by reason of failure to pay any poll tax or other tax.

Section 2.   The Congress shall have power to enforce this article by appropriate legislation.

Amendment XXV (Ratified February 10, 1967)

Section 1.   In case of the removal of the President from office or of his death or resignation, the Vice President shall become President.

Section 2.   Whenever there is a vacancy in the office of the Vice President, the President shall nominate a Vice President who shall take office upon confirmation by a majority vote of both Houses of Congress.

Section 3.   Whenever the President transmits to the President pro tempore of the Senate and the Speaker of the House of Representatives his written declaration that he is unable to discharge the powers and duties of his office, and until he transmits to them a written declaration to the contrary, such powers and duties shall be discharged by the Vice President as Acting President.

Section 4.   Whenever the Vice President and a majority of either the principal officers of the executive departments or of such other body as Congress may by law provide, transmit to the President pro tempore of the Senate and the Speaker of the House of Representatives their written declaration that the President is unable to discharge the powers and duties of his office, the Vice President shall immediately assume the powers and duties of the office as Acting President.

Thereafter, when the President transmits to the President pro tempore of the Senate and the Speaker of the House of Representatives his written declaration that no inability exists, he shall resume the powers and duties of his office unless the Vice President and a majority of either the principal officers of the executive department or of such other body as Congress may by law provide, transmit within four days to the President pro tempore of the Senate and the Speaker of the House of Representatives their written declaration that the President is unable to discharge the powers and duties of his office. Thereupon Congress shall decide the issue, assembling within forty-eight hours for that purpose if not in session. If the Congress, within twenty-one days after receipt of the latter written declaration, or, if Congress is not in session, within twenty-one days after Congress is required to assemble, determines by two-thirds vote of both Houses that the President is unable to discharge the powers and duties of his office, the Vice President shall continue to discharge the same as Acting President; otherwise, the President shall resume the powers and duties of his office.

Amendment XXVI (Ratified July 1, 1971)

Section 1. The right of citizens of the United States, who are eighteen years of age or older, to vote shall not be denied or abridged by the United States or by any State on account of age.

Section 2. The Congress shall have power to enforce this article by appropriate legislation.

Changes

(1) Changed by the Sixteenth Amendment

(2) Changed by the Fourteenth Amendment

(3) Repealed by the Seventeenth Amendment

(4) Changed by the Seventeenth Amendment

(5) Changed by the Twentieth Amendment

(6) Changed by the Sixteenth Amendment

(7) Changed by the Twelfth Amendment

(8) Changed by the Twenty-fifth Amendment

(9) Changed by the Eleventh Amendment

(10) Changed by the Eleventh Amendment

(11) Repealed by the Thirteenth Amendment

(12) Changed by the Twentieth Amendment

(13) Changed by the Twenty-sixth Amendment

(14) Amendment Eighteen repealed by the Twenty-first Amendment

11111111 the view of American statesmen like Daniel Webster, Thomas Jefferson,

In a national radio address on February 23, 1934, Huey Long unveiled
his "Share Our Wealth" plan:

Cap personal fortunes at $50 million each.

Limit annual income to $1 million each.

Limit inheritances to $5 million.

Guarantee every family an annual income of $2,000 (or one third the national average).

Free college education and vocational training.

Old-age pensions for all persons over sixty.

Veterans' benefits and health care.

A thirty-hour workweek.

A four-week vacation for every worker.

Greater regulation of commodity production to stabilize prices.

Long charged that the nation's economic collapse (Great Depression) was the result of the vast disparity between the super rich and everyone else. A recovery was impossible while 95 percent of the nation's wealth was held by only 15 percent of the population. In Long's view, this concentration of money among a handful of wealthy bankers and industrialists restricted its availability for average citizens.

Long believed that it was morally wrong for the government to allow millions of Americans to suffer in abject poverty when there existed a surplus of food, clothing, and shelter. He blamed the mass suffering on a capitalist system run amok and feared that pending civil unrest threatened the democracy. By 1934, nearly half of all American families lived in poverty, earning less than $1,250 annually.

—Huey P. Long (1934)

APPENDIX D

Economic Bill of Rights

"We have come to a clear realization of the fact that true individual freedom cannot exist without economic security and independence. Necessitous men are not freemen. People who are hungry and out of a job are the stuff of which dictatorships are made. ...a second Bill of Rights under which a new basis of security and prosperity can be established for all—regardless of station, race, or creed."

Among these are:

The right to a useful and remunerative job in the industries, shops, farms, or mines of the nation.

The right to earn enough to provide adequate food and clothing and recreation.

The right of every farmer to raise and sell his products at a return which will give him and his family a decent living.

The right of every businessman, large and small, to trade in an atmosphere of freedom from unfair competition and domination by monopolies at home and abroad.

The right of every family to a decent home.

The right to adequate medical care and the opportunity to achieve and enjoy good health.

The right to adequate protection from the economic fears of old age, sickness, accident, and unemployment.

The right to a good education.

"All of these rights spell security. ...I ask the Congress to explore the means for implementing this economic bill of rights—for it is definitely the responsibility of the Congress to do so."

—Franklin D. Roosevelt (1944)

KIRKUS REVIEW

A concise, well-researched argument against the dangers of unregulated capitalism.

In this brief but informative book, Gaasvig argues that America is a democracy only in name. "When any nation evolves to the point where the government and a majority of the wealth of the nation are concentrated in the hands of less than 1 percent of the population, no longer is that nation a democracy," he says. In the age of the Occupy movement, that view isn't exactly novel; indeed, many of the points made here will be familiar to even apolitical readers, anchored as those arguments are in the author's standard progressive belief that unfettered capitalism is causing a divide in this country between the haves and the have-nots—a division, the author says, that is both morally and economically suspect. What makes this book unique, however, is its orderly, educational tone. In what amounts to a clear-cut guide to social democracy, Gaasvig makes both economically and politically based suggestions for how to rectify the situation. As for the former, he recommends a range of initiatives, from publically funded child care to nearly guaranteed employment to what he calls a "three-party economic partnership" among capitalists, workers and the government. Politically, he suggests disbanding the Electoral College system and imposing term limits on members of Congress, among many other ideas. He also writes eloquently about voting and education. Critics may accuse Gaasvig of touting pipe dreams, but he clearly knows his stuff. With even the most idealistic of his ideas—say, the implementation of full employment with livings wages and benefits—he actively addresses opposing views in a controlled, logical way. And he is not unaware of the task ahead, particularly when it comes to inspiring the masses to be involved in the process. However, it's debatable whether the book will appeal to the American "majority" he references throughout, since this fairly erudite work can at times be a repetitive read. Nevertheless, for students of political and economic theory, it will serve as a factual, well-composed dissection of an extremely important topic.

A handy guide to the uses and abuses of capitalism.

26442549R00134

Made in the USA
Charleston, SC
06 February 2014